THE TICK OF
TWO CLOCKS

Also by Joan Bakewell

The Centre of the Bed: An Autobiography

The View from Here: Life at Seventy

Belief (editor)

All the Nice Girls

She's Leaving Home

Stop the Clocks: Thoughts on What I Leave Behind

THE TICK OF TWO CLOCKS

A Tale of Moving On

JOAN BAKEWELL

virago

VIRAGO

First published in Great Britain in 2021 by Virago Press

1 3 5 7 9 10 8 6 4 2

A CIP catalogue record for this book is available from the British Library.

ISBN 978-0-349-01393-0

Typeset in Perpetua by M Rules
Printed and bound in Great Britain by Clays Ltd, Elcograf S.p.A.

Papers used by Virago are from well-managed forests
and other responsible sources.

Virago Press
An imprint of
Little, Brown Book Group
Carmelite House
50 Victoria Embankment
London EC4Y 0DZ

An Hachette UK Company
www.hachette.co.uk

www.virago.co.uk

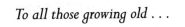

To all those growing old . . .

CONTENTS

Can you believe that all that turned out to be *then*? At the time I thought somehow it was *now*. Did it occur to you that it was going to be '*then*'?

Deborah Eisenberg

Introduction

I am in my eighties and moving on towards the end of my life. It is a time to think about things as they were and as they are now. How has it happened? Was it all inevitable that it should be so? How much have we shaped our own lives? And are we doing it still, as we move on through our last years? Or is choice an illusion, and are our expectations circumscribed by forces beyond our control?

This is a story of personal choices, many of them trivial. But each of them intended. It is a story of how I thought I was in control of numerous considerations, and found I wasn't. It echoes my thoughts looking back on life, our vivid sense of individuality set against implacable forces of character, change and evolution. It seems we matter little in our time or any other. Like the water in the stream, it flows but remains the stream. We are such.

I have lived through years of change: political, ecological, scientific, social. I was born into a time and place where my sort of people, lower middle class, had no phones, no cars, no foreign holidays, no expectations. All that has changed. It was a Britain of deeply rooted class divisions in a country of proud imperial power, where church and Parliament issued the rules and we were expected to obey. That has changed too.

I grew up believing the world around me was the norm: the 'now'. That norm would be how we judged what came next. Growing older, we discover that what we knew as the norm of power and wealth has been superseded by what came next. We have become 'then'. In the 'now', young people take for granted university education, global travel, things to buy and enjoy, choices of entertainment. But that too will change and evolve, and become their past.

This is the story of decisions I made about moving house, how the details of that move have built into something that has changed my life, moved it on to where I am now.

I am of a generation who almost accidently got rich: I bought a house in the 1960s and sold it some half a century later. It was windfall, unsought but more than welcome. It takes care of moving house, my old age and the care I will need then. There was nothing planned or intended.

I am well aware how grossly unfair this is. But that's how the housing market was as we entered this century. As property values boomed and our bricks and mortar turned to gold, I began to think there should be a tax raised on property that had soared in value. Then, I liked to imagine, we could improve social housing, do something about those sleeping rough – all the social aspirations we pay lip service to. But it's not a popular idea: it lacks what they call political traction, and would be a quick way to lose an election. It seems that people are nourished by hope throughout their lives, and hope of increasing their stake in the world is one of them. Now we seem to guard our assets with ever more fervour, as though some malignant force might snatch what we hold dear, away from us and our families. I can sympathise with that too. A sense of insecurity is one of the deepest anxieties that afflicts old age, which should be a time of calm, of reconciliation and resignation.

But old age also needs a project. We all need a reason to get up in the morning. Life provides plenty of reasons: to earn a living, bring up a family, pursue the loves of our lives, follow our interests – chase after football, art, travel. Serious old age changes all that. Instead, and slowly, the lifelong compulsion to do something – to be active, to achieve – wears away. Or perhaps as with macular degeneration: the eye's retina gets tired and doesn't work as well. Get up and go is for the young. The boisterous energy, ready to conquer worlds, is gone for good. We either conquered worlds or we didn't. It's too late to start now. That is of course a matter for gentle regret.

There are far more things we have failed to do than most of us have done. The sense of hope and possibility is now tinged with autumnal decline. I will never be an ice skater (Sonja Henie haunted my teens) or a brain surgeon. I will never climb high mountains (even Everest is too crowded these days). I will never sail across the Atlantic, design a dress, or run a bank. The wilder notions of what we might have done pile up beside us, bestow unwittingly a sense of melancholy.

But, like many older people, I have had the luck and health to feel I could create my own future. Since my Sunday-school lessons to 'do good, be good' and my resolve to make it to university, I have tried to make the most of what were not always easy circumstances. I have a career that might look like steady progress through the institutions of broadcasting. In fact, it wasn't like that at all. There have been lurches from one path to another, unanticipated switches between television and newspaper journalism, with snatches of novel-writing and stage-performing in the mix. It's been fun, and hard work.

There have been good reviews and bad, a clutch of awards.

Then, with all this, has come an un-looked-for bonus. Having begun to write about growing old, in 2008 I was invited by the Labour government to become their Voice of Older People, a role in public life, unpaid but amply rewarded by the insights it gave me into the lives of others. It happens to people with any kind of public profile: the invitations to sit on boards, become trustees, ambassadors, patrons. Such roles have their own kind of life: an abundance of paperwork – accounts, policy, company structure – attendance at meetings around big tables, and the friendship of all sorts of people, each of them expert in their own discipline. Eventually I fetched up as a Labour peer in the House of Lords.

Along the way I have two happy marriages — seventeen and twenty-five years apiece, failing eventually for immediate reasons. Two children and six grandchildren. Having escaped the unhappy and dysfunctional family of my childhood, I have grown to appreciate the value of a close and happy family life. In old age it comes to have a special intensity. It has sustained me most particularly throughout the pandemic lockdown and its isolation. Now I face deep old age, and charting the route and sharing it helps me on my way.

I

Plan

I should be making plans; that's what I'm told. I know it's true.

Plenty of people do make plans for their old age, and even for their deaths. 'Do not resuscitate' is a very clear plan: an instruction to medical staff about how you want to be treated in a crisis.

I know people plan, because I made programmes about them doing so. *We Need to Talk About Death* ran on BBC Radio 4 for three years. (Ironically, it was dropped from the schedules in the year the coronavirus arrived.) We discussed how to make wills, who to have at your bedside as you die, who will know your passwords when you've gone. As I was making the programmes, I knew it all applied to me, far more than to the younger production staff. But I kept that thought at bay: not me, not yet, surely. After all, I will have time to think about my own decisions when I've reported those of others.

There are other plans too: plans that seem to have come from nowhere and have taken many of us by surprise. Brexit, Covid regulations, vaccine availability . . . What bearing will they have on decisions the old are making for themselves? Decisions about our lives can be swayed by political change far beyond our control.

———— ∞ ————

As I've grown older, I've come to take more notice of my body, to heed the creaks and groans, notice the ills and spills. The mind might be vague, but the body is exact.

I listen to my body more keenly than my thoughts. When it complains, I do something. Usually I ask for advice.

My home was a four-storey Victorian house with my bedroom on the third floor, up four flights of stairs. As people far younger than me puffed their way to the top, clutching their chests and breathing heavily, I told myself, vainly, that the stairs were keeping me fit. But then my hip started protesting. I listened.

I went to see a consultant about the trouble it was giving me. She was very clear about what was wrong and what could be done. She was also elegant and attractive, and a woman. Why should this influence me to heed her the more? But it did. My body sat and listened, but even then I was reluctant to decide. 'Perhaps,' I said, 'I'll come along for the replacement hip in a year or two's time.' She was patience itself: 'When will that be, do you think?

You're in your eighties already.' I had the operation a few months later.

———

So now, in the list of things to deal with, it is the turn of decisions about housing.

Anyone over sixty needs to think long and hard about how they might spend the next forty years. Old age is no longer a blip in the calendar, a few declining years before the end. Old age is now a major and important segment of life: it should command as much thought – even anxiety – as teenagers give to exam results and young marrieds to planning their future.

The options of where to spend old age are plentiful if you care to look, though they often sound the same. Words like 'retirement' and 'care' crop up a good deal. How those words translate into reality makes a big difference. There are retirement villages and retirement homes; there are care homes and nursing homes: they each offer something different.

In my days as the government's Voice of Older People, I visited many, always with my inner eye watching for what might sway my own decisions. My favourite, for the breadth of its vision, was a retirement village in Hersham in Surrey, called Whiteley Village.

There used to be a grand emporium in Bayswater, London – the term 'department store' just doesn't do it justice. It was called Whiteleys and was conceived to be beautiful, with glass domes and wrought-iron railings – an Edwardian triumph, now Grade II listed. It was the proud creation of William Whiteley, a visionary philanthropist who, when he died in 1907, left plans and money to create a charitable trust offering housing and care for some 450 older people who could neither afford to buy nor rent their own homes. The grand emporium has now fallen to property developers, but his legacy remains in Whiteley Village.

I arrived through handsome brick gate posts down a wide drive that wound between cottages, roses round the doors, small front lawns. The housing consists mostly of what they call almshouses: individual accommodation, with more particular care as residents grow older and infirm. The village has a written constitution that invites residents to create and enjoy their own activities.

What is outstanding is that this is still primarily for those with limited means. To apply, you need to be in receipt of the state pension and entitled to housing and other benefits, with very limited capital assets of your own. This is actually conceived for those who really need it! You can come from any part of the country, and have to have lived in the UK for a minimum of five years. Such a place has the air of retirement utopia, all that older people might need with as much or as little socialising as you choose.

Why aren't there more such places? If William Whiteley can do it, where are today's visionaries? Who is building villages on their rolling Scottish estates, or their extensive acres? We know the state falls short when it comes to providing social care: a sequence of governments has promised to do something about it. So far: nothing. That has left many old people living in poverty.

There is room here for philanthropists. So step forward those of you who appear in the *Sunday Times* Rich List, those of you who are salting away untold millions in tax havens abroad. There is scope to leave a benign and lasting legacy: your name spoken with love and gratitude for centuries to come. Think about it!

Care for 'the needy' was once the duty of religious orders. That took a hefty blow in the sixteenth century, with Henry VIII's dissolution of the monasteries, but their surviving provision exists today in many of the country's almshouses. There are some two thousand of them in Britain, their common purpose being to offer accommodation for those in need. I became an ambassador for the Almshouse Association in 2020.

Each is a registered charity and many are sited in historic buildings. The Charterhouse in London is perhaps the most famous: an historic complex near London's Smithfield, which started life as a Carthusian monastery in the fourteenth century and provided the largest burial ground in London, to meet the needs of the Black Death. By the sixteenth century it was a Tudor mansion, and its owner Thomas Sutton set up not only a famous school, but a foundation to provide for eighty poor 'brothers'. Today it still offers accommodation for the over-sixties, forty older people in need, both men and women. Each has a small apartment of their own, but they eat communally, enjoy a library and volunteer their help as gardeners and guides. There's also some private rental accommodation, and a few rooms for independent residents in an on-site care home: it was here that the theatre director Sir Peter Hall spent his last months. Others who have sought solace at the Charterhouse include the novelist Simon Raven (if you've read his books you'll understand how he came to be penniless!). Syd Cain, the art designer who created many of James Bond's gadgets and designed several Bond films, died there aged ninety-two. Among those residents still vigorously alive are Michele Wade, doyenne of Maison Bertaux, London's oldest patisserie; an actor who used to be in *Dr Who*; and an illusionist who formerly lived with a pet leopard in Kensington. (The leopard had to go.)

The oldest of Britain's almshouses is probably St Oswald's in Worcester, which dates back, some say, to A D 900. Documentary evidence certainly goes back to 1268. Today its Victorian Gothic rebuild offers accommodation to some twenty-three residents. Almshouses are an important part of the housing mix, offering homes for life, usually with a care package provided by the local social services. They are a rare but precious option for those looking to make their final move.

———⊗∞⊗———

New Oscott Village is not any kind of rural idyll, but another bold and imaginative way to provide for old people.

It is run by a charitable trust, in partnership with a housing association, on the outskirts of Birmingham. There are 260 apartments, some of which go to those who depend on social care; others are rented or purchased. That's the residential provision. But there's more. This vast conglomerate of modern buildings also has a café, bar, restaurant, craft room, gym, indoor bowling, a greenhouse, IT suite, a hairdresser, laundry, library, village hall and shop. It is built around a street open to the public. The whole philosophy is that you can grow old enjoying as varied life as you choose or opt for seclusion in your own apartment. I met people who have done both.

There are other possibilities:

Retirement homes cater for people still active in their old age but also provide for those newly retired who wish to live among older people and benefit from the care they offer. The issue in the years when I was visiting was whether retirement homes should have a live-in caretaker. Someone to keep an eye on the building's residents. The matter became a hot potato as managers tried to save money by cancelling such jobs and depending on technology instead. Not surprisingly, residents wanted a human being they could know and trust. I saw the way the wind was blowing. With the advent of new technology – and it has become more pervasive since those days – mild supervision will be left to gadgets with buttons and robots. It's clearly a matter of convenience rather than preference.

I also saw accommodation for those who had become

frail and were being looked after in care homes. At the extremes of frailty I noticed those with dementia were often lodged on the top floor, presumably to give them privacy away from disconcerting noise and activity. In many cases, I met dedicated professional carers, usually women but not always, people who loved their work and got great satisfaction from it. One year I presented the Great British Care Awards at a posh London hotel. There I spoke with many who told me of the rewards of their work, how despite the low pay, limited chances of promotion and brutal working schedule they grew fond of the people who depended on them.

In my role as government spokesperson, I had the chance to visit a wide variety of places: even homes where they had string quartets in the evenings. I went to see the Mary Feilding Guild, when it was still a non-profit home in Highgate that offered accommodation and care for individuals who still wanted an independent lifestyle. The celebrated writer Diana Athill spent her last years there, until her death in 2019. I was curious to know how she had had made the transition from her own place to her comfortable but not ample room. The hardest part, she said, was disposing of all the things she had accumulated over a long life. That resonated with me: I knew that such a problem lay ahead: it affects most of us. Even those with a placid and uneventful life accumulate stuff, simply by not throwing things away. It will prove a continuing dilemma. Sadly and suddenly, in

March 2021 this beloved home was bought by developers who gave the sixteen residents, aged eighty-five to 104, three months' notice to quit. The last pensioners left on 7 May. No one is safe.

And then there's co-housing. I'm hugely in favour. I'm surprised the concept hasn't swept the nation – actually, I'm not that surprised when I think about it. Housing needs land, building, planning permission. Need I go on? This country simply isn't set up to recognise a bright idea and make it a reality. Certainly, over recent decades we've come to fetishise land and who owns it. There was a time when it was rumoured supermarket chains bought up motorway sites, not with the intention of developing them but simply to deny them to their rivals. It's a mindset that diminishes all concept of the public realm or public good. If these carried their weight in national planning, then co-housing would be up and away. As it is, it's slow to catch on. Yet it answers so many needs I can't but believe its time will come.

Co-housing originated in Denmark. It offers a different form of living and owning from the familiar house/flat/castle variety. In co-housing, each member – it is very much a community project – owns their own private living space, but they also share common spaces with others: laundries, gardens, community rooms, kitchens. The whole is more integrated than retirement villages and almshouses. This makes for a very supportive community. When several generations co-house together, care for the young and the old can be solved on site. Loneliness is avoided. Privacy is respected.

———∞———

The architectural whimsy known as the granny flat has become part of today's social planning. I have seen a number: they are usually neat, self-contained, cleverly adapted to maximise small spaces. And they are where you can be monitored by the children, or at least by one of them. The problem is not so much the space and the provision but dependence on the family.

Family relationships shift as we grow older, as one generation gives way to the next. This has to be managed with tact and tolerance: it is fraught with compromises and disappointed expectations. I remember the pang of regret I felt when, being too old to cope, I passed the task of overseeing the entire family Christmas hoopla to my children: I would cease to be the general and they my foot soldiers. I could no longer manage our traditional Christmas meal, with all its fancy accompaniments – giblet soup, chestnut stuffing, brandy butter – that I had set as the template decades before, or at least not without getting harassed, overheated and ratty. My children, too, were eager to display their cooking and organisational skills. It was their turn. They inherited some if not all of my foibles. I hope I conceded gracefully, just making sure they stopped short of sitting me in a remote corner with a rug over my lap and a glass of sherry in my hand, while they laughed and joked together in the kitchen. I could still — despite protests — peel the sprouts.

But there is no way that living close together all year round is simple. The bigger the house the easier, but even aristocrats with spacious mansions used the dower house on their estate to dump granny. Living alongside your family puts tolerance to the test, and it can fray at the edges. Minor irritants can become major at just the point when the weakening flesh needs closer care, until by the end they could be more than thankful to be shot of you entirely. It may be your favoured option, but it will call for amazing tact and ongoing doses of unqualified love.

That leaves 'independent living'. It's a phrase the social services are keen on right now. And they're right about much of it. It's good for morale, health and sociability if old people can fend for themselves. I decided to be one of those.

I know people who move house every few years. It has advantages: there's no time to build up the abundance of stuff that I will soon have to dispose of. They can renew their style, even get to know themselves a little better. But there's a downside. Do they have time to put down roots (not just in the garden), get to know the neighbours, establish relationships with doctors and schools?

I lived in my home for fifty-three years. I had begun to think of it as my inheritance, the place I had created and would leave to my children and they to theirs and so on into the history books. I can see why aristocrats and gentry do it: a sense of a permanent place in the world that bears the mark of the family's quirks and foibles, their history, their taste and way of life. Their furniture, even. I recall Alan Clark's quip that Michael Heseltine was an arriviste because he'd had to buy his own furniture! This remark by the scurrilous political diarist, the son of the great art scholar Sir Kenneth Clark, himself the son of a cotton-thread magnate, reeks of a snobbery that seemed to infect my own dynastic ambitions. What am I thinking? Perhaps my love of nineteenth-century fiction had imbued a sense of property as identity. A lifetime's memories cling to the house. I am both reluctant to go and eager to be off.

Mine is the story of a privileged move, from a big house to a small. But at any age changing places, giving up the old, is a watershed.

Through some shrewdness but much luck too, I had a house to sell. This puts me in the position of having choices and though I know that I am not unusual in this, I also know there is a smaller percentage of those like me who can make their own decisions. I am lucky. Choice is a privilege.

I try to decide what it is I want. I know there must be space for books, for paintings, for music and for having people round for supper. But what kind of space will it be: long views of the distant hills, or next to a clutch of shops, convenient for when I run out of milk? A wide and spacious garden, or a balcony for pots? On a road with a bus route but noisy traffic, or a country lane where there's still space to park a small car? I try visualising myself in each, but always come back to what I already know: city life with green spaces. It is interesting to me that most of us, when we make this final change, want a place with a strong semblance of what we are used to.

Most people hug the area they know. According to a 2019 government survey, 70 per cent of people moved to less than twenty miles away. In London, the distance was even smaller. Even of the remaining 30 per cent, most removed to within eighty miles. People in the countryside are even more likely to stay put. In the same survey, 90 per cent of country dwellers moved to less than twenty miles away.

I know I am going to be no exception. I share this reluctance to abandon what I know, what is familiar, where I have learned to feel at home. Now is not the time to chase some idyll of a cottage in the country with roses round the porch or a villa on the Med with sun loungers round a bright blue pool.

I am persuaded of this not by friends and the media, but by some arcane tribal instinct to belong somewhere.

My house seems to tell me not to move too far away, to stay close to home.

2

House

Here I stand, a tall house in a square in Primrose Hill. I arrived in what felt like a frenzy of building going on around about the time Lord Palmerston was prime minister and Florence Nightingale was off to the Crimea to see what difference she could make. Quite a lot, it turned out. But news travelled slowly: no one around here paid much attention, unless they had soldier sons fighting. Even for them, it was too distant to count. People's interests were mostly local.

In the 170 years since then, I've lived through some changes and families. The most recent lot stayed the longest, some fifty-odd years. The young family arrived with a small baby, an Austrian au pair and little money. But they were very happy, loved my tall windows and high ceilings, didn't worry about carpets or furniture much. He had a BBC job, so they looked to be settled and even prosperous one day. In the end it didn't quite work out like that. After a good few years there were bouts of shouting and hurried phone calls taken in secret. Eventually there was a divorce. By then they'd had a terrific seventeen years: drinks parties with lots of smoking, ashtrays in every room; children's birthdays in fancy dress; dinners that were all lit candles and fancy menus. I came into my own too: admired, even envied. It felt this was my heyday.

I was given listed status in the 1970s when I became part of a conservation area, so I couldn't be demolished. My walls can't even be tampered with too much, or the heritage folk will kick up a fuss. Fortunately for my family, they had turned my attic into a bedroom before the rules applied. It meant that their teenage daughter could shut herself away there and play rock music very loud . . . but that's decades ahead.

People have always been coming to Primrose Hill. Once they came to stand among the grasslands, pointing out the dome of St Paul's Cathedral in the distance. Nearby there was a scattering of settlements, the villages of Hornsey, St Pancras, Euston and Camden, between them a farm or two, plenty of stables for the huge number of horses needed by people down in the city. Slipshoe Lane, as one street was called long ago, hints at just how muddy the place was.

There was also Chalk Farm Tavern, still probably the most renowned and respected building hereabouts. It's just a two-minute walk away, though its history goes back way before my time. In the hullaballoo surrounding the murder of the distinguished magistrate Sir Edmund Berry Godfrey in 1678, his body was found dumped on Primrose Hill and taken to a local hostelry then known as the White House. By the early eighteenth century there was an inn registered as the Chalk House Farm. And the same place, by then called Chalk Farm Tavern, soon had a thrillingly scurrilous reputation. It was where duels took place, where shifty men up to no good came together to challenge each other. The injured took refuge in the tavern itself; their entourages sought comfort and anonymity. Duelling was against the law.

The place also boasted extensive pleasure gardens, with a bandstand, for some reason known as the Chinese orchestra, and a dance floor for some thousand people. Pleasure gardens were where people looked for fun before televisions and cinemas came along. Their provision of food, drink, music and lively company made them popular and noisy, so this was far from a rural idyll when developers came calling.

Mostly, the land on the lower slopes between Hampstead village and London had been the property of a number of major landowners; Lord Southampton was one. He sold up his estate in 1840, giving developers scope for what was to come.

But the most significant owner was Eton College. They caused a good deal of fuss when the Birmingham to London railway began to push its way into the city in the 1830s. They haggled hard over the deal.

The great railway boom brought sudden, even violent developments, and for the country at the time there was nothing more thrilling. Up in Yorkshire Charlotte Brontë bought shares in the local company, and helped get her wayward brother Bramwell a job as a station master. In 1830 William Huskisson, President of the Board of Trade, was killed while presiding at the opening of the Manchester to Liverpool railway; this stuff was new-fangled, and people didn't know how it would work.

As both the railways and people rushed to London, more and more people needed homes there. My foundations were dug in the 1850s. Above an ample basement and a spacious coalhouse, where sacks of coal were delivered through a hole in the pavement, rose four floors of spacious Victorian rooms. Other building sites were busy round about. Irish navvies (the term sounds abusive but was originally a professional name coined in the eighteenth century to refer to navigators building the canals) were brought in to dig the railway into Euston; they lived in rooming houses and hostels. Railway cottages were built for the men working on the line and all the railway staff too: signallers, porters and ticket-sellers. Alleyways between the swathes of grander houses, to which I belong, were home to all sorts of artisans – chimney sweeps, farriers, carpenters, hackney-cab owners, smiths. It was teeming with life and change, without order or planning.

One particular business flourished in the streets around me: piano-making. Piano factories were scattered in places still familiar today: one over near the large railway shed known as the Roundhouse; others across what would be renamed Parkway; down Gloucester Avenue and in Fitzroy Road; one at the junction of Gloucester Avenue and Oval Road; more at Eglon Mews and in Erskine Mews – piano-making enterprises proliferated here, there and everywhere. Mostly they survive only in the historic records, and as one or two conversions: a housing association here, a book publisher there. I like to imagine the sound of music reaching in through my tall sash windows. One of the factories produced Collard & Collard pianos, one of which would many years later grace my ground-floor room, submitting to the plonking sounds of children's music practice.

Certainly, the people who first lived in my square were respectable folk, the type of Victorian families who assumed a piano was part of their tasteful furnishings. In the 1870s, No. 1 was home to a doctor, with a large family who took in lodgers, but only of the most respectable kind: 'high-class Japanese families who were sent over by their government to study English', the records say. In the 1880s, an irascible philologist lived at No. 3: Frederick J. Furnivall, who also had a big voice in the world of Shakespearean scholarship.

Not far from these genteel surroundings or the celebrated Chalk Farm Tavern and its boisterous reputation was the more benign but wretched Boys' Home, built in 1865 when Victorian consciences were stirring. It was for 'the Training and Maintenance of Destitute Boys not Convicted of Crime'. Dickens would have recognised the sort of place.

Over the decades the mood and style has changed, echoing the social changes of peoples and purpose, but the memories of the past remain in the very buildings.

Again, it was the railways that pressed on. Curious and excited crowds gathered for the opening of the celebrated Primrose Hill Tunnel. They cheered its pioneering role in Britain's industrial growth: few thought it was anything but good. (They say a grumpy poet/printer working in Lambeth had been sending out sheaves of alarms and omens decades before, but they were too mythical and fanciful to catch much attention . . . at least for a century or so.)

But two blights followed hard upon: smoke and soot. More people crammed into smaller spaces were burning coal in open hearths. I had two open fires on each floor, so a lot of smoke billowed from my chimneys. Smoke was depicted in cartoons and paintings of the time as a sign of prosperity and well-being.

Then yet more railways tracks were built to serve the invading numbers. External walls fell victim to the dirt from Euston station. Inside houses, soot clung to curtains and plush furnishings, darkened porches. It lay in black lines along pediments, corbels and parapets. It happened slowly, but little by little the glamour of pristine new buildings faded behind a layer of drabness and decline. I began to feel the days of my prime were over.

And then came the fogs. By the mid nineteenth century London was well established as the most successful and largest city on earth. There was a pride in its appearance that went with its success: the early fogs were even praised. Darwin wrote of there being 'a grandeur about its smoky fogs'. And artists loved them: Monet came over from France especially to catch the image; Conan Doyle and Charles Dickens clothed their plots in fogs; 'smoke [. . .] is the London ivy', the latter wrote in *Bleak House*. There was a mystery and excitement in being unsure of the way home, people clinging together in the shared thrill of being almost lost.

Over Camden way, not yet central to London's huge sprawl, the fogs were not as dense or black. Or as dangerous as down in the city, where fog could kill: in 1873 there were reported seven hundred 'extra' deaths there due to the fog, nineteen of them people walking into the Thames, the docks or the canals.

The railways brought along another consequence. The increasing numbers who now worked in the city had to be found homes nearby. Gradually proud houses like mine, once home to single prosperous families, were broken up and became rooming houses for those who needed to live near where they worked.

The term rooming house entered the language at the turn of the century. It isn't used much any more, but just such a lodging is the setting of Harold Pinter's play *The Birthday Party*, with the landlady, Meg, providing motherly love for her tenant, the mysterious and reclusive Stanley. Such establishments round about often had several families living on a single floor, making do as well as they could, sharing kitchens and bathrooms, and enjoying a lively social life in the growing number of pubs around.

With people had come traffic. In the streets hansom cabs grew in unregulated numbers. Spaces throughout Camden were given over to mews and stables. There was noise and dirt; farriers and cabmen finding work and lodging above where vehicles and horses were stowed. When motor traffic came along, these mews slowly became what estate-agent parlance called 'bijoux residences'. And so it went.

Then, in the 1950s, another shift. In the years after the Second World War Chelsea and Hampstead had become, alongside Bloomsbury, hubs of intellectual life. Mayfair and Belgravia were already rich and would remain so. Successful writers and composers, academics and those 'bohemian' in their lifestyles, sought out the hilltop villages of Highgate and Hampstead, Yehudi Menuhin, George Orwell and Louis MacNeice were among them. For the less well off, the search for affordable places – run down and in need of renovation – intensified. It was my large sash windows and the high ceilings that caught the eye.

But I had other attributes too, of which I remain proud. My staircase runs in a continuous line from the ground-floor hallway up through three floors. Beside it a banister of polished mahogany flows in a continuous curve. Even at the steepest twist in the stair there is no break in its rising continuity. Some skilled craftsman had fashioned it to be useful and had made a thing of beauty. There is a single join in the long reach of the wood; otherwise, on and upward goes this graceful line. It was taken for granted, of course. Inhabitants get used to their surroundings and only really register them when they go wrong. In my case, the polished wood would one day gather the sticky sheen of children's hands as they went up and down to their bedrooms. It took a steady application of vinegar to remove it. And only then did my occupiers remark, 'You know, that really is a lovely banister.' But who notices staircases, unless they're in royal palaces or on Hollywood sets? There would be no dramatic gestures on my slight, but perfectly proportioned, presence.

Mind you, there were incidents. The walls were thin enough to hear those who lived next door, especially a brawl on a Saturday night when raised voices – a drunken man beating up a screaming woman – descended from the top of the house, floor by floor, bounced all the way down to the ground level. He shouting, she screaming. My recently arrived residents listened with horror, wondering what to do. But this was before there were such things as women's refuges or laws against domestic abuse. They discussed ringing the police but, cowards that they were, and knowing it would simply be dismissed as 'a domestic', they did nothing.

If no one noticed my banister, everyone noticed the friezes running around my high ceilings. They had been there from the start, crisply shaped with Grecian key patterns and floral curlicues. So admired were they that, decade after decade, different occupiers painted them white to brighten them up. Doing so and doing it regularly gradually blurred their sharpness until they became merely a series of bumps around the edge of my ceilings. Much later, during a major refurbishment by my long-staying owners, they thought about restoring the friezes to their former glory. It would take, they were told, high-pressure water treatment working foot by foot to dislodge the years of accumulated gunge. The cost was prohibitive. They decided not to look upwards but to take pleasure in the banister instead.

But I'm getting ahead of myself. In the mid-50s, a clutch of impecunious graduates had come seeking work in London and a place to live. I was pretty shabby and unappealing by then, but an enterprising developer who made a business of buying up the shabby rejects took me in hand, and gave me lick of cream paint and an olive-green door. 'Follow the olive-green door' was something of a mantra for new arrivals copying the trend set by young architects who were riding the boom of the post-war design revolution.

My basement had been made into a self-contained flat in the early 1950s, a dark place with narrow corridors and small windows looking out onto a dingy paved garden. On the right of the garden loomed a large factory, mostly occupied by a manufacturer of plaster ceiling fittings (had he supplied the ones of which I am so proud?) and a couple of artists' studios, one of them used by Paul Huxley, who was later to be a Royal Academician. The basement was leased by a retired couple who could not afford anything more prestigious: their style, accent and behaviour suggested that they were used to better than this run-down and shabby neighbourhood. But they would make do, hoping to command some kind of dwindling respect.

And that is where I come in. I moved in to the house in Chalcot Square in 1963, with my husband and our three-year-old daughter, pregnant with my second child and with our Austrian au pair in tow.

3

Us

The flock of Oxbridge graduates arriving in the 1950s brought with them the values and talents of their education.

Alan Bennett was one of the first to arrive, setting up home in a housetop flat in Chalcot Square. Sylvia Plath and Ted Hughes were briefly at No. 3. Others settled nearer Camden Town, creating a community that would over the years be the subject of cartoons, memoirs and reminiscences. Jonathan Miller and his wife Rachel moved temporarily into a basement in Regents Park Road and were there when Michael Bakewell and I moved into the area. Claire and Nick Tomalin had taken the same route from Cambridge to Camden and were living in one of the gracious Victorian houses in Gloucester Crescent; Jonathan and Rachel would soon move to the same street. Jazz singer George Melly and his wife Diana were soon there too. As was the philosopher Freddie Ayer with his journalist wife

Dee Welles, the artist David Gentleman and his family, and that of director Stephen Frears and editor Mary-Kay Wilmers. Alan Bennett and 'the lady in the van' now lived opposite. All this created a nexus of media and literary folk increasingly aware of their own particularity. Their contemporary, the cartoonist Mark Boxer, created a regular strip for the *Listener* called 'Life and Times in NW1', charting the lives of Simon and Joanna String-Along, a couple of knockers-through-walls. In 2018 Jonathan's son William would publish a memoir, *Gloucester Crescent: Me, My Dad and Other Grown-Ups*.

In Chalcot Square my husband and I set about creating our own self-contained world in our first real home. We had little money, so couldn't afford either carpets or curtains. We had to make do with shutters and wooden floors, unwittingly pioneering through necessity a style that would become widely popular.

And we made structural changes. We took our first venture into the world of serious architectural choices.

We wanted an attic room for our young daughter. Boldly we hired an architect rather than simply ask a builder. A ladder, a pulley-driven trapdoor and tongue-and-groove walls did the job. Our architect put the paperwork through the local planning authority; it wouldn't pass muster today.

And then there was the fire. My daughter was at primary school down the road, my baby son in his pram on the doorstep. It was mid-morning and I was sitting sipping coffee with the cleaner. It was a windy day and the trees were lashing and rattling. But soon there was another rattling: it came from the water pipes. Was the washing machine on? Had we overloaded it? Were we running too many appliances at the same time? We waited for it to pass. It didn't. I went to find out what it was. As I went up the stairs the rattling was subsumed by a roar. At the second bend in the stairs it was clear the top of the house was ablaze. I went further up to see how much hold it had. I stood facing the au pair's room and watched the white paint blister on the door.

Does anyone ever ask quietly for a fire engine? I yelled and yelled – so much they sent two. We heard them coming from miles away. Meanwhile I grabbed silly things from the children's room – a huge toy donkey, a summer hat – then fled. Outside in the square a small crowd had gathered. They stood back respectfully, as though the fire was mine and so was the catastrophe. Firemen went stomping past, two loads of them, towards the top of the house. Soon water was cascading down the stairs (by now we had carpets!). I got twitchy just standing watching. So I decided putting out fires was thirsty work and went to the local off licence to buy a crate of beer for the firemen. They were there most of the day, chasing down smoking embers, tracing where the fire might have started. The house – our precious home – was in ruins.

I don't remember the weeks that followed. I know we didn't leave the house but slept on mattresses among the awful smell of cooling embers. Neighbours rushed to help with the children while Michael and I found out how to put a house back together again.

Everyone offered the consoling 'well, at least no one was hurt'. Of course that's true. Obviously so. But I learned other things too. Homes matter in their own right. Humans endow their bricks and mortar – their thatch, cobb, wattle and daub, glass and steel – with part of their own humanity. It is beyond challenge that our human bonds are the very essence of our lives. But lower down the hierarchy of identity comes the place where we live. We bless it with our taste, our care, our pride and our love. Think only of the empty characterless homes of the unhappy; think of the colourful ephemera around street sleepers. Fires have been engulfing forests and homes of Australia; bombs are falling on homes in the Middle East; refugees are taking to boats, driven from home and safety by conflict and need. One of the fundamental things we do is create and build homes. It is a human need. Now I am alone, contemplating abandoning the one I have created and enjoyed for fifty-three years.

—⊷—

I needed to share the secret; I needed to tell someone. Only when I'd done that would I know it was true. Though I believed I wasn't leaving home, but rather planning to take home with me.

We go through life knowing lots of things within ourselves, truths we share only with ourselves, which have no exposure in the outside world. When they are shared, they take on a harsh reality. So who would be the first person I could tell?

Like many old people, I live alone. This makes major, life-changing decisions like downsizing tricky, to say the least. You have to do everything yourself. There is no partner to consult; no one whose life is closely woven into your own. But having had the thought, the impulse to confide in someone grows strong. I needed to choose the right person.

Children? Mine are grown and have families and mortgages of their own. How was I to know to what extent they brooded anxiously as to how I would grow old and what demands that would make of them? Did they view the prospect with alarm; look forward to any possible windfalls that might come their way; nurture worries about who would get the candelabra and have the courage to junk all my archive? I had no idea.

I had already scattered a few clues. Musing generally with friends on our taste in houses among addicts of *Grand Designs* and *Location, Location, Location*, I'd regularly made it known that I favoured one day landing up in 'just one large room, a sort of warehouse, attic kind of thing with space for a kitchen, a bed, all on one level'. I'd add decorating touches, 'perhaps bare brick walls, distressed paintwork, bare timber floors'. People would nod and ignore. So what, I would imagine they'd think, she lives on five floors with carpeted stairs – not much self-awareness there. Hmm, time to change that.

Friends? Not yet. They'd probably gossip with each

other. In the friendliest way, but there'd soon be phone calls, emails. In no time my cover would be blown.

But why was I keeping this secret? What was I afraid of? Did I expect to change my mind, was I fearful of their judgement, their advice? No. I knew what it was: I wanted to keep my decisions untainted. I didn't want suggestions or advice, however kindly meant. I wanted them to be 100 per cent my choices, my preferences, my style/taste/judgement. For the first time in my life it would be so.

Between the internal decision and the expression of it to the world at large, there is that shadowy place of decisions half real, half fantasy. I went round hugging the knowledge to myself. I felt like a child again: 'I am thinking about something you don't know.' Only when I began to believe in my decision did I feel it was time to nudge it out into the real world. I phoned a neighbour.

What makes a good neighbour? The phrase 'cup of sugar' comes to mind, a shorthand way of defining a distant intimacy that allows you to borrow for any sudden and small need, to consult practical but not intimate matters and no deep personal involvement. This intimacy was forced on us when we all lived cheek by jowl in narrow streets, or several families together. It becomes harder as people live further apart, and besides many gave up sugar long ago.

This was how I found the neighbour I needed.

He is ideal in a number of ways. First, he is possibly the most hospitable of the residents of the square; he hosts the parties that hold the neighbourhood together. Its where

we meet and compare notes, check out the latest proposals from the council, worry about the churn of local
facilities – more and more restaurants, fewer basic food
shops – concern ourselves with the care of trees, the planting of daffodil bulbs, pledge our support for the library. I
have been invited there to welcome newcomers, to catch
up with old hands, to meet many of his numerous friends,
even to celebrate Burns Night – the full thing: the Saltire,
the grace, poems read aloud, the toasts. Not surprisingly,
my friend has a network of knowledge about the area that
answers exactly my sudden interest in what's up for sale,
who's on the move, what might one day become vacant. I
ask him for coffee and advice.

It is the autumn of 2017. It is indicative of my ambiv-
alence about this move that I mix up the dates, setting
out coffee and biscuits on a morning no neighbour turns
up. He arrives the following week. I begin the tale of my
imagined old age. Not a moment too soon: clearly the
memory has lapses.

I tell of the ideal: I talk about that one huge room,
about loft spaces, old barns, refurbished churches, a place
without stairs but space for books, music, sofas for ageing
limbs, cooking informally for friends. It sounds too good
to be true. But why not? Start high: the market and money
will bring grim reality. He nods sympathetically, and does
nothing to dampen my hopes.

Explaining the long-term fantasy to the ideal neighbour,
I simply want to register my planned destiny with someone

who knows the turf. He is of course immediately practical. And I realise I have crossed a line. I thought I was sharing a secret; I was doing no such thing. I was proclaiming aloud that I was planning to move house. No, the ideal neighbour was not going to go gossiping around. But he was there to help, wasn't he?

Television's 'buying-and-selling' programmes can't fully convey the awesome weight of people's moving-house decisions; we are never made privy to their innermost thoughts but I watch greedily, hoping to catch an inkling. I share their hesitations, sympathising whenever they draw back from the abyss of change. Now I have my own decision to make, and I have just made it real. The starting gun, the flag, the whistle, whichever, has just set me on my course.

The ideal neighbour is in touch within days. He has already asked my permission to speak to our favourite estate agent. The term 'estate agent' usually makes me recoil in horror, waving garlic, but David is different. He set up locally many years ago, knows the history of Camden, the shifts of its identity, the force and energy of its civic societies. He loves the place.

David's account of the current state of the business is eye-watering. When he first became involved with the property market, in 1987, it was a matter of people coming through the door wanting to buy a home. He would listen to their account of what they wanted and tell them what he could offer. In those days many ordinary people could afford and find mortgages to help them. And the transaction went ahead.

World events changed all that. From the 1990s money poured into London: money in flight from Russia and Syria, later from Greece, Italy, Spain. 'We don't sell homes any more,' David tells me, 'we sell investment. Investors buy homes they don't live in; the rental sector is now huge. With the credit crunch, interest rates fell almost to nothing. People saw property as a safe haven for their money.' David tells me how many people buy one home, then another and another, renting them out to families who yearn to buy just one. From abroad, the rich buy new houses off plan, paying agents to let them out for rents that are not price-controlled. Or they simply leave them empty. Londoners know there are vast tower blocks and luxury estates that are hardly inhabited. Meanwhile the young can't raise the money to buy because all their earnings go on rent. Social housing is at a low ebb. The housing plight is a nightmare.

I have taken David my old-style request. I have a house to sell and I want one to buy. We oldies with our own homes are lucky indeed. The sale of the big house will pay for the smaller house, with probably a chunk of money left over. That's how downsizing works. It is how the better off among an ageing population can fund their old age. Yet there has recently been universal media shock at the notion of the old having to sell up. Headlines have shrieked their disapproval: 'Britain's care crisis: 300,000 pensioners forced to sell homes to pay for care bills'. Indeed that is what happens, because there is nowhere else for the money to come from. This outrage is based on a fundamental mis-understanding that assumes that social care should come free – like the rest of the post-war settlement – as a part of the NHS cradle to grave provision. It is not. It is why we have pensions when we pass pensionable age.

When such provisions were introduced, working people lived on average a mere two years longer than their pension age. It was judged that their pension, together with a few savings, would probably see them out. Now life expec-tancies are much longer: people can live some twenty-five years or more in retirement and their continuing needs for care – unlike their medical needs – have to be met from their own resources. Hence downsizing! Hence the outrage that mistaken expectations are not being met.

I am one of those fortunate enough to have a substantial property to sell. Like others of my generation who have had similar luck, I can look to the money sustaining me in my later years.

Everything is happening. Everything seems to move into another time zone. Having dithered over my anxieties, my fantasy plans, my secret decision, the cat is out of the bag and already beyond my control. The private has become public. People are acting at my behest.

David goes into action.

There is news.

It is both good and bad: there is right now a place for sale, just such a place as I had outlined over coffee. 'I know it's much sooner than you wanted . . .'

Everyone knows the feeling. You talk for years about buying a new car, about one day baking a soufflé, even about holidaying in Cambodia. It becomes a routine topic of conversation, eliciting useful advice – why not go electric?/ firm egg whites are the key/don't miss out on Angkor Wat. Soon there is exasperation from sharp and efficient friends that you can be such a ditherer.

I agree to go and see.

4

Buy

It's 15 November 2017 and I have an appointment to see the property on offer. But it is a dark and gloomy night. There is no one resident in the house – it is indeed a house – so I am escorted by David, my friendly estate agent.

David Birkett has already been a key player in finding the property. His is a local independent estate agent with a single shop and he likes it that way. His competition hereabouts includes the mega-chains. David mops up the rest of us, having found homes for Alan Bennett, Stephen Mangan and Harry Enfield. He is an estate agent like no other: shaved head, casual dress, a long scarf of coloured stripes wound round his neck and falling across a puffer gilet – no trim navy suit and white shirt for him. He has always been 'out' and will, as my sale goes through, be marrying his partner Jitesh Modha at Islington Register Office. He has been in the district since 1989, when it was still known as Regent's Park: Primrose Hill had not yet earned its own identity. Hc knows everything that's goes on in these several square miles. And I trust him.

The previous night I had been to the meeting of my regular book group. Being professional people of a certain age, we all have our own homes with spacious rooms, ample sofas, cushions and bookcases. I am alert to the fact that wherever I move, I will need to accommodate this regular event in my diary and the arrival of my reading friends.

Book groups are a remarkable social flowering in a culture that is moving towards electronics and internet media. Where did they come from? Were they prompted by a crisis in bookselling, invented by some bright PR person to save the sinking ship? Or were they a spontaneous response to the bleaker, more alienating times of consumer living? I don't know what others are like but my book group isn't in any way competitive; it nurtures a collegiate love of the same things: good ideas and stories well expressed.

Ours began some twenty years ago, and I still admit to a warm glow of expectation when I see 'book group' in the diary. Unlike most that are usually women only, our group includes men as well, primarily partners. We take it in turns to make individual choices and host the evening at our homes. Come the night we probably scramble out of daily woollies and slippers into something worthy of an appearance that is semi-public; smart-casual, the magazines call it. But the books are what matter.

Over the years I have been introduced to the novels of William Maxwell and Willa Cather, tracked Orwell in

Burma and tackled titles as challenging as *Wittgenstein's Poker* and *Freud's Wizard*. We have grown to understand what kinds of book choice will go down well. My own choice, *The Leopard* by Giuseppe Tomasi di Lampedusa, was among the most successful. Douglas Coupland's *J-Pod* did not make it. And poetry can present something of challenge Wendy Cope's acerbic topicality in *Serious Concerns* was an easy win; Don Paterson's *Landing Light* was tougher going. But it did trigger a memorable moment: a soprano among us with Orcadian connections recited his poem 'Zen Sang at Dayligaun'.

On the eve of my house visit, we had been discussing *East West Street* by Philippe Sands, the story of the town in Poland, Lviv, where his family had its roots. The tale leads on to the part a lawyer relation played in introducing the terms 'genocide' and 'crimes against humanity' at the Nuremberg war crimes trials. One of the book's many merits is the personal discoveries made by the author and the significance for him – a human rights lawyer – of the definition of these powerful and resonant phrases. It makes me more than usually alert to a sense of place, of home, of legacy. And of words, when shared with friends. My new home must be as hospitable to my reading friends as theirs already are to me. I bear that in mind.

――― ∞ ―――

The place I am to see is one of a group of artists' studios. In 1882 Alfred Healey designed a series of single-storey buildings, each with one huge window letting in wonderful light into one large room. Although he wasn't an artist himself, Healey had the notion that artists come together to share their calling, and more practically their accommodation, rent and gossip. It led me to think about how other artists had come together, and made art and history in doing so.

It has long been a truism of inner-city regeneration that where artists go, others will follow. Why should that be so? Examine it closely and it makes obvious sense. Artists are independent of spirit, often poor, seeking large spaces where they can work all hours and socialise with fellow spirits. Freedom and the space for creativity is most important. They bring character to an area at very low cost. No wonder others join them.

Van Gogh took the idea of artists coming together and pushed it further. He moved to Arles hoping the Yellow House where he lodged might become a colony for other post-impressionists. The only one to arrive was Gaugin, yielding to heavy pressure from his friend Vincent, and destined to stay only nine weeks. Yet in little more than those two months, van Gogh produced thirty-six canvases, Gaugin twenty-one, claiming 'a fever of work seized me'. It all ended badly as van Gogh's mental health collapsed, a seizure of rage ending with a severed ear, Gauguin's departure and his own hospitalisation. Later, in his memoir, Gaugin commented laconically, 'some things bear fruit'.

They had certainly borne fruit in the Lake District,

where William Wordsworth settled in Grasmere with his sister Dorothy, for 'plain living and high thinking'. At around the same time, Robert Southey (like Wordsworth a future Poet Laureate) and Samuel Taylor Coleridge planned to create the Pantisocracy, a utopian community of writers and their families. It never came to fruition, but their mutual support produced work that would create the Romantic movement.

In Paris, artists weren't so much looking for an ideal society as a shared passion for art and friendship. At the turn of the twentieth century a former piano factory in Montmartre was turned into twenty small workshops. The building was dark and dirty, and swayed in strong winds, earning it the name Bateau-Lavoir. From the 1890s it was home to, among others, van Dongen, Picasso, Juan Gris, Max Jacob and Amadeo Modigliani, later attracting the likes of Matisse, Braque, Derain, Cocteau, Apollinaire . . . the names go on. Artists all, seeking ideas and company. Later the focus moved from Montmartre to Montparnasse, where La Ruche – rebuilt from a structure created by Eiffel for the 1900 Exhibition – offered home and exhibition space to the likes of Léger, Soutine, Chagall and Delaunay. It still does so today.

It isn't just artists who tend to come together.

The Bloomsbury Group was mockingly said by Dorothy Parker to have 'lived in squares, painted in circles and loved in triangles'. The very name Bloomsbury maps out where the homes of the well-off writers and thinkers congregated.

Virginia Woolf and her sister Vanessa, their extensive circle of friends including John Maynard Keynes, E. M. Forster, Lytton Strachey and Dora Carrington, met and talked, wrote and had affairs.

Aldeburgh too, a small seaside town in Suffolk, became a hub for people of sympathetic interests: this time music, inspired by the composer and all-round musical genius Benjamin Britten, who with his partner Peter Pears set up home there in the 1940s. Others followed: Imogen Holst, Colin Matthews, Oliver Knussen. After his exile from the USSR for his active defence of Solzhenitsyn, the cellist Mstislav Rostropovich and his wife, soprano Galina Vishnevskaya, would later find a home there too. The Aldeburgh Festival was created in 1948: since then the air has been full of music – orchestral, choral and operatic.

This tendency of creative spirits to make their homes in a particular area spreads further than a few houses and studios. It infects the neighbourhood. Florence in the fifteenth century, Vienna since the early twentieth, Liverpool in the 1960s: each city has taken on the character inspired by those artists who made it their home.

But does this congregating of the like-minded go further? To what extent does like intuitively seek out like? If it is the natural tendency of human society to do so, then what are its social and political implications? Is the coming together of such groups of artists a template for race, money, language? And what promise does that hold for multicultural communities sharing their differences and enriching the lives of each?

Minority communities come together for the sense of solidarity it gives them in an often-hostile setting: Asian families in Bradford; Portuguese, Irish and Polish districts of London. Socially there are divisions too: young people often flock to the livelier parts of cities, some pensioners seek the calm of country villages. Push this further and you develop a sense of proud and even belligerent nationhood, with pressure from strongly identifying communities as diverse as Wales and Scotland to seek independence. Right now there are movements for local independence across the globe: Catalonia, Corsica, the Basque Country in Europe; peoples further afield seeking a land of their own freedom, among them the Kurds, the Tuaregs in Algeria and Mali, the Ashanti in Ghana, the Bedouin in North Sinai. There remains the painful failure of Biafra to break from Nigeria. Such impulses are powerful and visceral. Their global and political ramifications will be with us for a long time to come.

And the thought started because some artists wanted to come together.

—◈◈◈—

The front door opens onto a narrow corridor. The lighting isn't helpful: the space looks gloomy and we have approached the single-storey building down a dark alley. It could be the opening of a menacing movie: there is little colour, little light. It isn't doing much to sell itself, because the woman who last lived here has died and her family are supervising its sale from a distance. There is a stale smell of a room long unoccupied, and air of quiet neglect that, left any longer, could fall into decay. But I have that kind of prickling sense of anticipation that animals must have when they scent a quarry or an attacker. The space is indeed as I have specified to David: one big, embracing room with smaller spaces branching off.

I stand and stare. There are ample sofas around the unlit and cold fireplace – no mantelpiece, I notice; a dark wood dining table with chairs; and a French window of small panes that has a 1930s feel to it. I peer through the glass at what appears to be a muddled space beyond, unfocused, unused. I can only get an impression of size, not of any kind of garden, no flowers, no lawn, no colour. I can see the remnants of a shed collapsing on itself, and the murky waters of a sunken pond. It is dispiriting to look at. I turn away and consider the room itself. The walls are so muted that they lack any character; the carpet is neutral too. I am scratching round to identify any personality of the owner. I find it in the paintings: there are plenty of them, hung in the 1950s style, side by side at a single regular level. They suggest the tidy, regular mind of an owner who let her spirits loose enough to enjoy the room's only colour: great splashes of red and blue, easy watercolours of places perhaps she knew. The paintings endear me to its owner, even though her taste isn't mine. She loved and collected paintings, quite appropriately for an artist's studio. I soon learn and am fascinated by the fact that this was the studio home of Arthur Rackham.

I knew about Rackham, read books with his illustrations to my children. He was not one of the towering names of the Pre-Raphaelites, for whom I have always had a rather overheated regard, but rather belonged to the lower slopes of the imagination. His career was as a creator of drawings for Victorian books. As such he was brilliantly skilled. His illustrations for *The Ingoldsby Legends* and *Gulliver's Travels* were popular at the time and are still widely known. Many of his watercolours and sketches were destined for art galleries worldwide. But it was a limited ambition.

When I go back home, I look him up. In 1903, when he was engaged to Edyth Starkie, a former student of Henry Tonks at the Slade School and by now a portrait artist in her own right, her rather grand Irish family dismissed Rackham as 'a tuppenny-ha'penny Cockney artist'. Rackham had indeed been struggling to make a decent living. The Boer War, he believed, had inhibited his kind of illustration: 'the camera was going to supplant the artist in illustrated journalism, and my prospects were not encouraging,' he wrote years later.

Arthur and Edyth married not far from me, at St Mark's Church, Hampstead, in July 1903, and after a honeymoon in North Wales – amusingly, they had chosen it for the fishing but apparently were disappointed, catching nothing – they moved in the September of that year into Primrose Hill Studios. I have a vision of them standing on this very threshold over one hundred years before, newly-weds and artists.

The studio scarcely met their needs, as he wrote in a letter to a friend: 'We want the addition of a bedroom and dressing room and I think it can be arranged by a balcony in the bigger studio and part of the underneath shut in. It will give us a queer compact little place with no room to spare, but I really think we could manage if there was a family for a few years as another tiny room could be cut off the studio under the balcony.'

I am having the same response: yes, I could manage as it is, but I would like to make changes. And then I realise that I have already decided, virtually at first sight, that this is the place for me.

I come back within three days for a second viewing, this time by daylight. Although it is winter, bright light pours through the huge windows; I notice rows of books in unexpected places. I warm to the departed owner. And to the space.

But I am hesitating. Not because there are things I don't like about it, but exactly because there are. It's exhilarating and frightening at the same time. There are things that I would wish to change; the many small panes that make up the sizeable window would have to go. There is a confusion of small rooms of no determined purpose that would need defining. There is an awkward staircase to a half-landing, and an inadequate bathroom. I know all this can be changed.

I hesitate because it is a moment for hesitation. This will be it. Not just for the next phase of my life, but until the end. I am acknowledging that I am looking for somewhere I can stay until I die. That feels momentous. And maybe that won't be that far ahead. I am, after all, in my eighty-seventh year. What will life be like here as I grow older, feebler, less nimble? What will it feel like when my working life comes to an end and I am more isolated, and often alone? Will it be quiet enough? Will it be too quiet? Do I want – for the first time in my life – to be responsible for a serious garden? I know that many older people move house because, as they tell their children, 'I can't cope with the garden.' A garden running wild distresses them. It is proof they are no longer in control. I shall need to have a garden suited to older ways, older limbs. Is this it?

David has soon exhausted things to point out to me. He can see I am in internal conversation with myself. I decide to – as they say on the quiz – phone a friend.

A few days later I have lunch in a café round the corner with the writer Andrew O'Hagan, who lives in one of the other studios in the group, not quite opposite but near enough to lob a tennis ball. He has a keen mind and is a canny observer of people. He tries to restrain his enthusiasm, but it none the less spills out: 'Look, I know enough about you and your life to know this will suit you exactly.'

It is, as he tells it, a uniquely congenial community: 'We all know each other. We're all on calling terms, friendly but not too intrusive. We help each other out: knock on doors for help or delivered parcels . . .' He goes on, gently but insistently describing what my life would be like. I welcome what I hear. My confidence grows. I am about to decide.

A day later I phone David Birkett: 'Yes, I want to buy it.'

━━◦◦━━

A new report has been published, detailing the lives of older women, and it's shocking news.

In February 2010, the independent review chaired by Michael Marmot, Professor of Epidemiology at UCL, published the report 'Fair Society, Healthy Lives', that concerned itself with reducing health inequalities in England. It told how people living in poorer neighbourhoods would on average die seven years earlier and spend more of their lives living with disabilities than those in richer neighbourhoods. Housing, income, education and socialisation are all factors that make the difference. He added, for good measure, that health inequalities are largely preventable, and set out a framework for remedying the situation.

Now, in 2020, comes 'The Marmot Review 10 Years On'. The news is not good. For much of the twentieth century our population has enjoyed rising life expectancy. But from 2011 these improvements slowed dramatically, and have almost ground to a halt. Improvement in life expectancy had continued thanks to things like the smoking ban and the sugar tax. But now the tide has turned. In some of the more deprived areas outside London, life expectancy has actually fallen. Especially for women. Yes, women are dying earlier than their mothers did. What is happening?

The UK had been a world leader in dealing with health inequalities. Its impetus was fired by the pioneering work of Victorian philanthropists, Lord Shaftesbury to name just one, but our current government has failed to keep up the good work. Its policy of austerity engendered a precarious job market, zero-hours contracts, food poverty, homelessness, and a rental and housing crisis. 'This damage to the nation's health,' concludes Marmot, 'need not have happened.'

So, many women will be dying younger than they might have expected. Their prospects in old age are getting worse rather than better. It's unlikely I'll be one of them: I am middle class, with a steady, if wayward income, and a personal pension to supplement my state pension. I have lived and worked, and am now ageing, in comfort, a comfort many other women don't enjoy. I want it to be otherwise: health inequality is a blight on our civilisation.

And then came the coronavirus. It became known almost at once that the old would suffer the most. The Office of National Statistics reported that by 29 May 2020 more than 46,000 people had died from coronavirus in England and Wales and that more than 4 in 5 were aged seventy and over. Looking at the number of deaths per thousand, there is an even more stark finding: in the group aged 60–69 fewer than 1 in 1000 had die from coronavirus; age 70–79 it was 2 in every 1000, in 80–89 7 in every 1000, aged 90 and over 18 in every 1000. These figures, quoted by Dr Elizabeth Webb of the Age UK Research team, referred to those living in their own homes and did not include those in care homes. The government's ill-judged moving of older patients from hospitals into care homes without their being tested brought about an avoidable surge in deaths. The evidence suggested that people aged fifty and over were not any more likely than younger people to catch Covid, but that, having caught it, the old are likely to have a more serious experience. Thus, for the foreseeable future, the prospect for health in old age has another negative factor to take into account.

5

Sell

My house now goes on the market. David warns me it is not a good time for selling: winter, pre-Christmas and the market stymied. There is a sense of tension in the air, a mix of uncertainty surrounding the approach of Brexit. All our lives are affected. Unless I sell, I can't buy. David commissions a glossy brochure with photographs so impressive I can hardly recognise my own home. Yet they do not lie: I have simply cleared away books, clothes, coffee cups, books, more books, papers, and after fifty years living there I suddenly appreciate the house all over again. A low angle and a wide focus have done the rest. The description features flattering words: superb, distinguished, potential, renowned, excellent. Even the pokey garden, festooned with golden leaves at their most lyrical, looks inviting. That is of course the idea: to invite people to see. Within a few weeks some twenty prospective purchasers will have visited.

There's a sense of being stripped naked, of being exposed to public view. Will they — whoever they are — sneer at the personal quirks of my decor, the incongruities of my rooms? And will I care? Long ago I regularly resisted invitations from David Frost, who as host of *Through the Keyhole* asked people to turn their homes over to television cameras, for a celebrity panel to guess who might live there. I feared the false intimacy of such exposure. Now it has become a necessity.

Appended to the sales pitch is something I have never seen before. It is called an Energy Performance Certificate and is a single-spaced document of many colours setting out the potential for saving energy costs. Who knew? It promises wonders: potential future savings of £3771 over three years. Top actions you can take to save money: mostly wall and floor insulation. Again, who knew? Certainly not me. The paper is headed HM Government, so why was I never sent it? Such is my woman's instinct to self-blame, I begin to wonder whether I did indeed receive it and threw it away as some unwanted marketing leaflet, or even a takeaway menu. Yes, perhaps I am to blame for not saving £3771 over three years. Imagine what I could have done with that: a lavish tour of India, perhaps; the purchase of some rare but beautiful object; the rental of a cottage in France for the summer . . . I succumb to regret and self-pity. Why did no one tell me?

Well, no one did, and no one will. That's how this complex, multi-stranded life works.

My strategy is to leave David to do the sell: I don't want to be around feeling self-conscious about my scuffed chair covers and chipped door paint. I don't want to witness some high-tech wizard sneering at my sound system or watch some foodie looking down their nose at my 1960s Kenwood. So I either hide in my favourite café round the corner and gorge on chocolate brownies or head for the House of Lords to share my misery at the state of the nation with congenial colleagues. Primarily, I stay out of the way.

But there is one exception, and who wouldn't do as I did? It takes nerves of steel to deliberately avoid meeting and greeting one of the world's most glamorous actors. I stay for the visit of the Film Star.

It's hard to describe how one responds to meeting a 'living legend'. I met the Queen once; she was full of smiles and charm, brilliant at saying just enough but not in any way joining chummily in a conversation. As she passed on to speak to others in exactly the same tone, I felt well, yes, there she is, that's the Queen. It was a moment not like any other, but then not that special either. What had I expected? The Queen is totally consistent and reliable: it is a great quality that is never mentioned. It's not possible to detect whether she is having a rough day or feeling particularly upbeat. She is totally on the job in hand, effectively briefed so as not to seem ignorant, but we each know we are merely one in the procession of her lifetime of encounters. For a fleeting second, we have her total attention and then she is gone. And nothing has happened.

Likewise, the Film Star. He has come to view my house. I am at my desk, working. He is looking round. We exchange pleasantries and nothing more. He goes. And nothing has happened. What did I expect?

He didn't change my life and he didn't buy my house.

But there is interest. By early April the deals are coming into sharp focus: the sale of one house, the purchase of another are coming right. By which I mean that, as advised by David, the two transactions will meet the equilibrium he had set out at the start. A young family will be the new residents of No. 20. Like many others who live hereabouts – and indeed like movers everywhere – they are not moving far. The family come round for drinks; they talk of the changes they are planning. I am delighted. I think, were they to keep my home exactly as I had lived in it I would feel the strands of nostalgia tugging me back. As it is, they will, given abundant planning permission, be creating a transformed home of their own: to house, they tell me, their two sons and their grand piano. I rejoice to know family noise and music will be resonating in these old walls. Of course it cannot be any business of mine once I have decided to sell, but even so I feel a deep sense of relief.

Now I have to take on a role I have never wanted: I shall have to manage this project. Managing is not something I have ever wanted to do. I have no training for it. No inclination to acquire its skills.

Looking back, I can see I have done many jobs: waitress, shop assistant, receptionist, advertising copywriter, BBC studio manager. Finally I came to harbour as a journalist. The term embraces many activities. I have worked on radio and television, and been a commentator for several newspapers. So within one discipline I have followed a variety of jobs. Sometimes one job slides effortlessly into another. I think of writers: the novelists Fay Weldon and Salman Rushdie exercised their early talent with words and ideas as advertising copywriters; David Puttnam and Alan Parker flexed their film-making muscles in commercials. Such progress from one to another was predictable.

Over the decades I have seen the world of work change. In my grandparents' day their greatest aspiration was a job for life. Most of the working class found it: in the factories, the mills, the mines, or in service, as servants to the better off. They didn't switch skills throughout a lifetime. My grandfather was a cooper, making beer barrels in a Midlands brewery. When that brewery closed down, he didn't move to a different job in the same area. He went to his union, who found him another job as a cooper, but in Manchester. He moved the family to a new city rather than acquire a new skill in his home town. The same held true of my father's generation: he qualified as an engineer and worked in the same firm for over forty years. Within that time he worked on projects abroad, but never changed companies or skills. He ended up as managing director.

My father's generation had embraced something called

a career: the application of skills, rising up the ladder of promotion towards more money and authority. Many today still stay in the same company. The BBC is one. When I joined the staff as a studio manager at the age of twenty-two, they discussed my pension with me. I recall a bright spark of a trainee producer when I was a journalist on *Newsnight*, who decades later became, in succession, the BBC's Director-General, head of Channel 4 and then the president and chief executive officer of the New York Times Company. Single-direction career triumph.

But work since the turn of the century has changed a good deal. The world has become more fluid. There are no jobs for life: even if you own the shop there is no guarantee it won't go bankrupt. With the decline of traditional industries in the 1980s, people woke up to the fact that where there had once been a reliable place in life with the security of a job, a roof and even a pension, life was more risky, even hazardous; ask the miners, who went on strike for over a year in 1984–5 to save their jobs, and lost.

Retraining – or re-skilling – grew into a regular option. The Open University was established in 1969 to offer just such training. Birkbeck College, London University, which was founded from the Mechanics Institute movement begun in 1823, offers part-time and evening degrees for people who have regular jobs. I am currently its President. More and more, such flexible learning, and online learning is coming to the fore. As the pace of technological change quickens, future generations will enjoy a sequence of careers. No point any more asking a promising grandchild, 'And what would you like to be when you grow up?' The answer may be 'everything'.

Pensioners might expect to be off that particular hook. Except more and more can and want to continue working. Finding jobs isn't always easy. Employers tend to favour younger applicants. But crises can create opportunities: the pandemic has called back retired nurses and doctors. Shifting patterns of education mean retired teachers now return to offer teaching back-up. Sometimes, needs must.

I knew from an early age that I didn't want to manage. I didn't want to organise the party games for my birthday. That was my father's job. I didn't want to plan the suppers for my teenage get-togethers. My mother would do that. Never having been willing to practise, my ambition wilted. It's good to start as you mean to continue: I was happy to let others take the worry and the responsibility. If you want to end up running Amazon, start by organising the toys in the sand pit. There'll be no looking back.

In part, I failed because others were micro-managing my life for me. My schoolmistresses were strict and exact: they controlled how I sat, stood, walked, ate. As head girl I was programmed to meet town worthies on the terms they set out. My parents were in control too: my handkerchiefs — remember those little squares of cotton edged with lace or embroidery that we filled with snot? — they had to be ironed and stacked in a neat pile, one that wouldn't topple over. I envied girls who took control of their own lives, but I couldn't break ranks without a fuss. My mother chose and bought all my clothes until I was a student, including the clothes I took to Cambridge with me. Only once there could I ditch the lot.

No practice, no formal ambition. As a freelance, I have lived by working at what I enjoyed. It has been a piecemeal career, not a steadily planned route of any kind. Now I have a project to manage: an actual ambition with a defined path. It is new to me. I am now a project manager. I know the mantra: 'deliver on budget and on time'. And you have to take the blame. That's what happens to managers. That's what managers are for: someone to organise, and then take the blame.

I look into the proper business of a management career. I hadn't realised how it has proliferated. We seem almost swamped for managers. It's the rung-of-the-ladder career choice for increasing numbers of eager graduates, perhaps dazzled by the legendary incomes of top managers, who morph into entrepreneurs the higher up the ladder they go.

As for the public sector, I can cite – without naming names, of course – institutions that seem micro-managed to within an inch of their lives. What's clear, even to out-siders, is that layers of professional managers take up layers of time. Government departments, NHS Trusts, academy chains, major charitable foundations – are they all run by people who've climbed the managerial ladder? Is the world over-managed, so systems collapse under the burden of their own weight and need to be broken up? I can think of some.

For fun, I look up courses and degrees in management studies. The curriculum lists the things you have to be good at. I take note:

- Setting short-term and long-term goals.
- Recruiting the right people.
- Ensuring the daily functioning of the enterprise.
- Delegating effectively to people with the right skills.
- Liaising across departments, conveying crucial information about the job.
- Motivating people to serve the job well.

It all sounds platitudinous enough, like Christian virtues. But judgement is in the execution. The penalty for going wrong will be heavy. And clearly things often do go wrong. They will.

But I know that if you can run a home, bring up children, cook and feed them, attend to jabs and health, plan holidays, get the car serviced, run rotas for Guides and piano practice, tend ageing parents, keep on friendly terms with teachers and neighbours, fix outings with your partner . . . you are a manager in your own right.

It just doesn't feel like that. I am in new waters here.

Team building: I like the sound of the phrase. But not the idea. I've never even employed my own secretary or

anyone as grand as a personal assistant. I am too impatient
not to think that I couldn't do the job better myself. I'm
also intimidated by someone swanning around my life, my
papers, phone calls, scripts, bills, parking fines, diaries,
files, answered letters, unanswered letters. I see them as
a pointing finger indicating my shortcomings, being, per-
force, polite about cock-ups, disappointments, mistakes. I
sense the dead-handed legacy of school and home.

I don't delegate, so lots of stuff doesn't get done, either
in the right order, as I hope, or even at all. I have been
the manager of my own life and am fully to blame for its
rackety course. But now I'm stepping on to a wider stage.
Lots of people do it all the time. That doesn't mean it isn't
traumatic. Indeed, it's so fraught with emotion and conflict
it provides material for several highly successful television
series – property programmes I love. I start to watch with
a keener eye than before, guessing at just what goes on in
those off-screen discussions about money, mortgages. How
do those transformations take place? Walls knocked down,
paint splashed, new kitchens – Phil and Kirstie can't do it
themselves. Of course not. They employ a team to do it. I
will need my own team. In my imagination I am beginning
to grow fond of them, even though I don't yet know who
they are. They will be shaping the home in which I spend
the rest of my life.

I will depend on the talents of others to help me through:
architects, accountants, bankers, designers, garden
designers, house-clearance experts, movers. It is my good

fortune, and perhaps a smidgen of good judgement on my part, that they turn out to be a widely diverse and friendly bunch: several nationalities, all backgrounds, ages and personalities. Primarily, each one is gifted with the skill and tact to get on with the others; the Polish builder with the toff designer, the hippy gardener with the skilled potter. What a mix: the best that Britain has to offer.

At the same time and in another enclosed world, the Conservative government of Theresa May will be putting through Parliament the European Withdrawal Bill, designed to thwart such a spontaneous coming-together of multi-national talents. The House of Lords, though much abused as unelected and unrepresentative of 'real people', is in fact a goodly mix of diversity and talent, peopled largely by wise and experienced individuals. There are former judges and ambassadors, top civil servants and former Cabinet secretaries, surgeons and entrepreneurs, a smattering of those, like me, from the world of broadcasting, film and the arts. On any day the debates will be better informed and more interesting than any of the self-serving exchanges in what we call 'the other place'. I find ideas and friendships in abundance. So I am moving from a world that is helping decide the future of nations to a small domestic enterprise that will only affect myself. From the chaos of a new house being transformed to the chaos of a House divided, I ricochet between the two. It is a giddy life.

Next to managing, there is something else I dread. Money.

I have always been conflicted, feeling I'd never get enough of it yet despising people for whom it's life's major ambition. Money. Ever since uncles pressed florins into my tiny fist at the end of their visits, I have known there is something subversive about it. Its abundance can provide us with everything we want; its absence can deprive us of everything we need. No wonder money has such a grip on the throat of society.

Getting old confronts us with specific problems around money. They are quite basic: will I have enough? Where will it come from? Will it meet all my needs? How will changes beyond my control affect my income and my way of life? Such questions haunt us all our lives and the answers change. Old age struggles with that. More than has ever been necessary before, hard sums must be done. Answers will be exact and precise: incomes will be a total of state pension, personal pension, savings, income from assets and, if any, current earnings. There will be help if we need it: the Money Advice Service was set up by the government to help us through the undergrowth. It is non-profit-making and impartial, by which I mean it is not selling you anything. Then there are advisory charities – Citizens Advice and such – to whom you can turn to for, well, advice. The initiative and the will to act comes at a time when temperamentally we are least inclined to bother. But bother is what I must do.

Even though my career choices have allowed me to

spend my life doing things I enjoy, of course they have brought money along too. But what I do with that money is surrounded by anxiety. The constraints of a frugal childhood haunt me still: basically, spending is wrong; saving is good. This of course endows spending with a dangerous thrill and makes saving smack of dull conformity. Which is why I get heady whenever shops stage their sales: spending combined with frugality equals virtue. I can't resist.

More recently and with the depredations and restrictions of the pandemic, the suffering of those without enough money to feed their families is something I am appalled to see in Britain. There is a pressing need to reshape our values to drive out such a scourge. It is almost eighty years since the Beveridge Report defined the five great evils that a decent society should overcome: want, disease, ignorance, squalor and idleness. Those huge community challenges are constantly frustrated by our individual needs and greeds. I see it in my own life, my own finances. A tepid contribution to charities and street homeless simply won't do the job.

I am haunted by an unhappy divorce that played out against my financial interests. I had, on my second marriage to a much younger man, put the ownership of the house, which had been exclusively mine for several years, in both our names. An act of misplaced trust, as it turned out. I also sold the cottage I owned in Cornwall to provide the deposit for a gamekeeper's lodge we purchased on a National Trust property nearer to London. With two working lives it made weekends in the country possible. But I bore the basic outlay.

English divorce law requires the sum total of the couple's assets to be divided equally between the two. So half the value of the house and half of the cottage would be lost to me. My lawyer argued powerfully and with some success that this was not an equitable settlement for what had been earned largely by my own working life. Nonetheless I found myself paying over large sums to be rid of a deeply unhappy situation, to buy out my ex. I have remained single ever since.

Now, twenty years later, selling that house is providing me with the wherewithal for the next step but these transactions have to be handled by experts. Then I have to decide what to do with the money left over. On to my team step those who know about money. They are a different tribe: they wear dark suits; they have crisp cuffs. They work in offices, their cars have spaces in the car park, they sit at desks, keep files, understand spreadsheets. When I stumble into their orbit they magic up cups of coffee from assistants, familiar with the regular routine. They are impeccably polite and patient with my short-term memory loss. They barely disguise their surprise at learning I studied economics at university. I feel safe in their hands, not because they deserve it – they do – but because I have decided to feel safe. Any alternative would trigger fits of panic and sleepless nights. I have made a decision to trust them because they know things I don't. And I need access to that knowledge. Not all of it, but enough to sign contracts and accept dates of exchange with confidence.

There is something gratifying about people having an area of expertise totally closed to me. As a jobbing journalist I developed a jackdaw talent for picking up odds and scraps of information on many topics. I can impress total strangers with an easy familiarity with the FTSE 100, rock formations in the Peak District, the plays of Lorca, only for them to realise as the conversation stalls that my knowledge, though eager, is shallow. Now I am dealing with experts: people with years of study and concentration to back up whatever advice they give me. Nothing shallow about what they will bring to my cause.

⸎

Meanwhile, I attend the House of Lords where the debate goes on. I am a passionate Remainer, so attending was by no means the relaxed commitment it often is. I listen to the arguments to and fro, and vote against invoking Article 50, which will launch us recklessly into the unknown. To no effect: the whole misconceived juggernaut lurches ahead.

However, the process does have a strange balancing effect in my head. When I am sick and tired of agonising over Brexit, I turn refreshed to concerns about my move. When decisions about the move begin to pile up, I turn with renewed energy to vent my spleen on Brexit. It's rather like being a student again, torn between the double strain of exam revision and a torturous love affair.

With none of the sex.

The suits bring on board other suits, to draw up legal documents. I shall never meet these people; perhaps being confined to offices they are not suits at all, but sitting at their ease in jeans and open-necked shirts. I like to think as much. But their documents don't read that way. We will speak on the phone and launch the process of moving monies around.

On 11 June we exchange contracts on both purchase and sale. Completion is set for late September.

Completion: it's a wonderful word. It suggests work well done, the moment to open a bottle and raise a glass. Congratulations all round. In house-buying, it comes at a price. Money in, money out. Or in many cases, including mine: money out, delay, money in. This calls for a bridging loan: another attractive phrase for an unwelcome necessity.

I now own the studio, so insurance has to be arranged. I consult with the company involved and am interrogated about its configuration.

Me: (confidently) It's basically a tall
one-room studio.
Them: How many floors is that?

Me: The front of the house has two storeys,
but the main bit is one ground floor.
Them: Then it's a bungalow.
Me: Well, it's taller than a bungalow, with
stairs. It's a studio.
Them: That counts as a bungalow.
Is it free-standing?
Me: (warily) Not exactly.
Them: Well, does it join on to
any other building?
Me: Yes, it adjoins the studio next door.
Them: Just the one side?
Me: Yes, the studio next door.
Them: Then it's a semi-detached bungalow.

I am the proud owner of a semi-detached bungalow.
It's official.

6

Change

I shall need the skills of an architect. And will enjoy what has long interested me: how and why people live in the buildings they choose, and what variety of taste and style shapes our cities. Many share my interest; we don't always agree.

The summit of Primrose Hill is a popular destination. There's almost always a small group of people at the top, outlined against the sky like teeth on a broken comb. They gather around the sign that points out all the buildings in the vista below: the horizon is very wide. On a clear sunny day you can discern – or you could before the pollution – the soft curve of the North Downs. Oohs and aahs greet the recognition of landmarks: the Shard, the Gherkin, the other towers of glass and steel that render the City of London much like any other seen from afar. I regret their homogeneity.

When I first arrived in Primrose Hill the one building that stood out proud and clear was Wren's St Paul's

Cathedral. It had the authority of uniqueness, signalling the great resurrection of London after the terrible 1666 fire. In the rebuilding that followed, Christopher Wren designed some fifty other churches throughout the city, many of which also survived the Blitz and are blessed with names like St Dunstan-in-the-East, St Olave Old Jewry and St Edmund, King and Martyr – more evocative surely than today's medley: the Cheesegrater, the Walkie Talkie.

In preparation for the work on my studio, I'm trying to focus, and articulate what exactly my taste is in buildings. I clearly don't like the all-out glass and steel of Canary Wharf, and my view of the city skyscrapers suggests a curmudgeonly oldie disapproval. But it's more complicated than that. My grandparents had a *Coronation Street* terraced house, my parents a mock-Tudor semi-detached; I own a spacious Victorian terrace. Each of these declares its taste and its class: upward mobility spelled out in bricks and mortar. But what do I actually prefer?

I have grown up liking buildings. I took the tram each day to school in Stockport and sitting upstairs learned the different styles and decorations of the shops, offices and municipal buildings along the route. None was inspiring. But the great variety was impressive. Who had taken trouble to design and produce such a tantalising selection of doors and windows? They are only rectangles after all. But generations of designers and builders have thought it worthwhile to elaborate on the crude oblong and give a twist of originality to this most banal structure.

The house where I grew up offered little inspiration: it was part of a ribbon development south of Stockport. It had stained-glass windows in the front door and pebbledash across the outer walls. Below that was red brick, against which I practised throwing a tennis ball back and forth, not just ten straight throws but the same number of times under-arm, under-leg, behind the back, with a pirouette between – the obsessive dedication of the lonely child. Perhaps I will find the same repetitive joys in my retirement. The front of that early house was separated from the back by a tall latched gate that demarcated the front as respectable and for visitors and the back half the plebeian area, where tradesmen called and the family came and went. Beside it was the coal house, as big as a small room and stacked with glittering black nuggets decanted daily to feed the single fire that heated the entire house. My memories, though vivid, have carried no echoing inspirations to be copied into my future homes. I was glad to leave it behind.

When I moved to London my eyes were even more eager to glut on the world around me. Travelling around by bus I always took a seat upstairs on the left. It is the perfect level to survey all the pediments of the capital's buildings, mighty offices and a gallimaufry of shops. Grander than the Stockport tram run, here the competing architectural practices had sought to leave their mark, earn a reputation and delight their clients. The result was largely anonymous: try as they might to be different, the effect is a row of routine buildings. Perhaps that is why we have come to admire the serried ranks of Georgian terraces, each alike and adding up to an inspiring whole. But, watching from my bus-top perch, many London routes reveal a happy – or disastrous – variety of shapes and sizes, arches, stairways, doorsteps, railings, knockers, letterboxes, entry-phones and proprietorial lettering.

I learned quickly that London's vast conglomerate of spaces covered a multitude of communities and styles, the biggest divide being between north and south. How did I come to identify myself as a natural north Londoner? Perhaps it was simply where I landed first. The route from the north arrives at Euston, after all. Perhaps it was sheer laziness. But I sense something more. North London has hills: Highgate Hill, Hampstead Hill; south London has plains, reaching only slowly towards the North Downs. And at a guess, I think north London has more greenery: the mighty spread of Hampstead Heath being north London's answer to the more manicured beauty of Greenwich Park: 'heath' and 'park' indicating the differ-ence. In the 1950s, when I arrived here, it was possible to recognise the different villages that constitute the whole: each nothing more than a string of shops that served a loyal community and gave a particular identity to the area. I had seen those localities spread out, reaching their tentacles towards each other and merging into an octopus whole that now has London in its grip. Chains of identical shops and eateries make Camden much like Dalston, Hampstead like Blackheath. Only the treasured centre – with its clutch of monuments and galleries, the Royal Academy to the Tower of London, the Houses of Parliament to Buckingham Palace – retains its stubborn tourist-glutted identity. Is this why, I wonder, there is such lack of identity among younger people, less sense of belonging, of loyalty?

Oddly, though I have lived in London for more than sixty of my eighty-seven years, I still think of myself as Stopfordian, with deep cultural roots in Manchester's history. When I became a member of the House of Lords I chose to be Baroness Bakewell of Stockport.

My own involvement with the building boom of the late twentieth century has been tangential, but it has been there. I served for several years as a judge for the Gulbenkian Prize for Architecture and was sent to different parts of the country to weigh up their nominees. I learned to look hard, and slowly to understand things like services, drainage, crowd flow, ventilation. Later I sat on the jury for the Tate Gallery (I was a founder member of its Friends group) to decide who of the world's best architects would get the opportunity to transform a disused South Bank power station into Tate Modern. This was a major responsibility: more learning about services, crowds, access and light. Some 148 architectural practices applied, and I enjoyed major presentations from, among others, Renzo Piano, David Chipperfield, Nicholas

Grimshaw, Will Alsop, Tadeo Ando, Rafael Moneo, Rem Koolhaas and the eventual winners, Jacques Herzog and Pierre de Meuron.

It was an absolute privilege. Day after day we sat and listened, questioned, debated. I wasn't always heeded: one suggestion I pressed without success was that the building should have a crèche for the children of those who worked there. In those days it wasn't rated a priority and my idea was rejected. When I wasn't struggling to keep up with the details – both practical and aesthetic – of their ideas, I took note of the architects themselves and observed the architectural dress code: grey, black and white; rarely any ties (this was 1994), a great deal of good cashmere, unobtrusive while being noticed. Architect chic, I called it.

The building aesthetic is always governed by materials and techniques. Today there is an abundance of both. The ideas that governed the Parthenon survive in the canon of architectural history, but no one seeks to copy it. Now there is rivalry between a generation of brilliant architects. With money and talent in abundance they seemed bent on standing out from the crowd. As a result, they created a crowd of their own. Richard Rogers took the services from the inside and put them on the outside of his Lloyd's building; Norman Foster shaped the Gherkin (officially 30 St Mary Axe) in ways that Michelangelo could never have dreamt. The trend to nicknames arrived, a popular putdown for mighty institutions. They are just offices after all. Rogers Stirk's Leadenhall Building became the

Cheesegrater, Renzo Piano's London Bridge Tower was always the Shard, Rafael Viñoly's Fenchurch Street building the Walkie-Talkie. Unhappily, this last tilted in such a way that the reflected sun melted cars parked in the street below, earning it the honour of being named the worst new UK building of 2015 by *Building Design* magazine. I see that the craze for individuality marked out a unique cityscape of its own. Who knows, one day it may be a tourist destination in the way the towers of San Gimignano draw visitors to Tuscany. Perhaps it already is.

Fired up by all this looking and assessing, I have signed up each year for Open House, the annual weekend when many cities – Athens, Lisbon, Chicago, Dublin among them – open up their best buildings and invite people inside. Thousands of us take to the streets and trek from building to building, passing each other along the way waving guidebooks and crying 'have just seen . . .' and 'not to be missed!' Over the years I have visited the Art Workers' Guild building in Bloomsbury and Lutyens houses in Hampstead Garden Suburb, seen inside the Bank of England on Threadneedle Street, explored and braved the dripping tunnels under central London that were prepared for government survival, had the Second World War gone against us. In 2020, the weekend's highlights included a converted chocolate factory in Hackney, a walking tour around Harley Street and Greenford Quay in Ealing. A passion for architecture means you are never bored. I certainly like looking. But what about actually living?

When I sought out my first flat in London my priority was to find somewhere that looked out upon greenery: I felt the need to be near parkland, mature trees, the possibility of daffodils in the spring. Inside, I wanted tall rooms and big windows. The small flat where I paid £5 a week rent had neither. But this new studio does: a tall, very tall ceiling, and, opening onto the garden, windows. I would like them to be even larger. The garden itself has a much-neglected pond and a mix of broken sculptures and overgrown flowerbeds. Like each new owner, I will want to make lots of changes.

But first I settle a few more pressing matters. I decide I do not want a bath. Those designing accommodation for the old should know that many of us don't use a bath, and with good reason. Stiffening limbs make it more difficult to get out of a bath: we risk getting stuck. I have a nightmare of indulging myself in some grand hotel, but then find myself unable to get out of the bath and am discovered there by the maid in the morning, stone cold like David's painting *The Death of Marat*, but without the dagger. So no bath.

Next, I plan for my carer. No, I don't have a live-in carer right now, nor do I expect to need one soon. But I'm thinking ahead. Realistically, there will come a time when I can't cope. I will reach the point that causes such heartache for single old people needing regular personal care but not wanting to sell their homes. I have the opportunity to make space – a small, self-contained bedsit – to accommodate a live-in carer. If more of us had such a space, there would be less pressure on care homes and the social services. But I know full well I am lucky to afford it.

Next: I understand how personal things are. It is a truism of those who make a habit of riffling through skips that the items most commonly thrown out by incomers are bathroom and kitchen fittings. People are picky about where they wash and where they cook. I notice this in the glossy-magazine coverage of celebrity homes too. Unless you are a megastar and always eat out, the kitchen is a busy and very active place, and highly personal. Families laugh and argue here; chefs get precious about the layout; people in a hurry need to reach quickly for what they need, those with time to spend want cupboards full of fancy gadgets. I am a bit of each of these.

Back in the 1990s, we had made a major refurbishment and commissioned a bespoke kitchen at No. 20: a second separate sink, open cupboard space beneath the hob for saucepans, an island with accommodation for bottles of wine. Perhaps what was special for me would not be special for the buyers of my house. I make an insolent move. I approach them and ask whether I can take it with me. I have a hunch that this kitchen, tailored specially to my needs, might well end up in a skip. (Incidentally, I recommend skip-watching to all those struggling to furnish a new home: amazing stuff turns up there. My son has salvaged several good doors!) So I ask to take it, lock, stock and barrel, to the new studio. They agree.

Next, the bedroom. My son, a qualified cabinet maker,

had created a run of wardrobes that accommodated in a series of cleverly arranged spaces virtually everything I wore. Could I take these with me too? Generously they agreed again.

It was time to confront the business of finding an architect. Despite all the grand names that I've let into this chapter, I didn't actually know how to find an architect specifically suited to me, the sort who would come within my price bracket. I couldn't conjure them in my mind's eye, apart from the architect chic of course. But I didn't know what kind of offices they had, whether whoever took me on would delegate the job to some less talented minion, to what extent they would press their own tastes upon me, to what extent this would lead to ructions. I need not have worried.

To find an architect, you can of course ask around informally. You can also approach RIBA – the Royal Institute of British Architects – which has some 3700 accredited practices. The unique quality of a good architect is their ability to think of solutions to problems that never occur to the rest of us. They also know how to handle planning permissions, and the constraints on conservation areas, greenfield sites and the greenbelt. That, and their experience of how to project manage is how they make – and deserve – their fee.

I found my architect on the hoardings of a house on a local street. I recognised it in a vague way, but without any clear focus. I checked it out. In fact, Chassay & Last had been in Primrose Hill – virtually round the corner – for a number of years. I knew they had a reputation, but I wasn't sure what for. I went online. I saw things I liked. That was it. As it proved, being a local practice was ideal. Later, they would come to see the drawbacks. Their help in steering racks of my clothes through the streets of Camden was certainly not part of the brief. But by then they were friends.

In fact, they were two – and Chassay was not one of them, having peeled off in the direction of Notting Hill some years before. They were Malcolm Last and Jill Facer, husband and wife who, I came to realise, had mastered the skill of combining their talents without rivalry or acrimony. Their view of the studio as it stood was that it was both a total muddle and a huge opportunity. I could see the muddle for myself, but the opportunity was theirs. They made the most of it.

Early on they are round at the studio, measuring and photographing. After several lively visits Jill and Malcolm offer me a chart: it is a schedule that sets out the coming year and promises a complete home in late summer. It is a neat diagram with colours indicating different stages on the journey: planning, preparing the site, building, decorating, etc. It looks wonderful and I take it to heart. I see it not as a proposal of how things might go if we're lucky but as a prediction of how things most certainly will be. Mistake.

Jill and Malcolm then get to work developing and detailing the plans, and we huddle around my dining table as I try to visualise their proposals. This is totally thrilling for me. I am a coiled ball of excitement; there are lots and lots of drawings and papers. Malcolm – architect chic, of course – quietly and with a slow smile makes what seem radical suggestions. They remain calmly tense as they wait to see whether I approve.

It's clear they have thought of creative ways of changing the space that I could never have thought of; ideas that delight me. The basic studio will be enlarged to accommodate my kitchen. What's more, they plan to transform the pokey-paned French windows into wide, broad sheets of glass, sliding open from floor to ceiling, virtually creating another room of my garden outside. Still on the ground floor, an enlarged bedroom takes in the wardrobes and has a tiny en suite, while what was a jumble of small rooms will be totally transformed into a fully equipped bedsit that will one day accommodate my carer; until then, it will be where my family and friends will stay. Malcolm and Jill also plan to open up two windows, giving me more direct light, and will move the two short flights of stairs – you would think this was impossible in what is technically a bungalow. You would also think no planning authority would allow such a thing in a listed building. (We shall see.)

Their ideas are thoroughly radical while at the same time retaining all the idiosyncrasies of the original studio that would matter to the planning authority. Camden, which has a wealth of varied and historic buildings within its span, has a keen eye for any trespassing on their rigorous planning regulations. They do this with the approval of

Camden's citizens, who are keen guardians of their neighbourhood and scrutinise the planning proposals that go up
on lamp posts with the attention a hypochondriac gives to
dosage instructions on tablet bottles. I am one of them: I
like to weigh up basement plans, parapet changes, rebuilding of terraces and garden sheds, even though I am neither
the owner nor the direct neighbour.

Planning permission matters: without it you are lost.
And penalised. Decades back, the chemist on the corner
had gone ahead with a simple extension to his attic: scaffolding erected, builders' buckets up and down, new windows
installed. No notice on the lamp posts. But at some point
late in the day the planners realised. I think the idea was
that once the planners saw what trouble had been taken,
what disturbance to the environs, what minor impact on
the skyline, what expenditure of effort and money, they
would concede and demand only minor adjustments. Not
so. They were absolute in their judgement. Up again went
the scaffolding, up and down again went the buckets; the
entire extension was dismantled. So I knew we were up
against formidable forces.

Planning authorities are normally regarded as an
obstructive hurdle to the legitimate wishes of homeowners
who, after all, are paying hard cash to fulfil their dreams.
To some extent, and especially in my own case, I am drawn
to agree. But I live in London and have always followed
with a beady, greedy eye when planning schemes go for
consultation and response.

I sometimes respond. I certainly take a view.

Over the year, I will have eighteen meetings with the architects. But I never set eyes on the planners. I am best out of the way. My jumpy eagerness to see the plans through might have raised hackles. As it is, I can follow the correspondence. The continuing theme is 'there is no harm to the historic fabric of the building'. The alterations – moving staircases, changing windows – will be allowed because they are not part of the original Victorian building, and it is this that is listed, not the twentieth-century alterations. There are some issues about the roof structure and a lot of talk about ties and soffits that goes over my head – literally, it transpires, as they refer to the ceiling. The planners' attention extends to the garden wall running along the alleyway that leads to the studio mews itself. The idea was to use bricks exactly like those of the studio opposite, thus creating a sense of harmony down the 'street'. But this is not allowed: we are to use second-hand London stock laid in Flemish bond. The planning application also specifies the pointing and type of mortar. And the replacement of a ventilation grille on the flank wall comes under question. So much attention to detail! I wonder who wrote the rules, and whether other local authorities bring such meticulous attention to planning and building regulations. Then I think of Grenfell Tower. Clearly not!

Most new houses in the UK do not use an architect. Most are built by construction companies to a standard design.

Latest Housing Ministry figures show an increase in 2018/19 of 241,000 new homes . . . from a low of 124,000 in 2012/13. The figures include homes created through change of use, including more than twelve thousand from former offices. In London alone there were 2777 office conversions. As patterns of living change beyond 2020, we can expect more working from home and more such conversions, using up redundant office spaces.

These conversions are problematic because developers don't currently need planning permission. So there are no quality or space controls. Developers don't even have to provide windows. Many create homes that are cramped and dark, unsuitable for family living. More worried about profit than aesthetics, they are adding to the drab architectural landscape of inner-city life. While the government pleads for more affordable homes, the charity Shelter calls for much more social housing. Both are badly needed. But who is worrying about the look of the place, the legacy we leave behind as typical of the twenty-first century? It won't be a good one.

7

Grow

On my first visits to my studio I had seen a garden of considerable size for London. It had an untidy and browning pond, some paving stones, a collapsing wooden shed and a tangle of unkempt bushes. The entire space was overlooked on a grand scale: the backs of a street of three-storey Victorian houses rising within twenty yards of the garden wall. The range of windows – lit up early on winter evenings – reminded me of Hitchcock's *Rear Window.* Each house has a rear extension; some gardens are decked out with garden furniture, barbecues. This is city living: I shall not be alone.

A garden has scarcely figured in my plans, but towards the end of life I find myself growing closer to the natural world. We do, after all, share the same life cycle: birth, growth, maturity, decline, ending. It is evident all around us in flowers, animals, trees. We see it more closely in our own lives, pets and gardens bringing comfort and a sense of the passing of the years. We realise we are part of a flow of nature, consoling, unthreatening. An early cancer diagnosis is a shock of terror; the death of a pet is a moment of sad reflection. We become reconciled.

It's odd then that many older people anxious to downsize give as one reason among many the fact they can no longer 'handle' the garden, that the standards of tidiness they have long applied to lawns and flowerbeds, planting and weeding are just too much for their arthritic knees and collapsing energy. The will is no longer there. I myself have long said that proper gardening feels like housework out of doors. It bears the same challenge to instil order, maintain discipline, expel the unwanted and tame the disruptive. I should remember my youth. Then I knew instinctively that when you embrace rather than defy nature you get reassurance and pleasure, even as the weeds invade and the grass grows.

My relationship with the soil, flowers and small creatures began when I was very young. I can remember causing panic and severe intervention when I put a handful of soil in my mouth. I also remember cries of dismay when I waved a worm in the air and watched it wriggle. Early on I was told that such things were dirty and nasty and not for nice clean little girls.

Instead my curiosity was channelled by my parents into bright shiny children's books. I grew up with the *Flower Fairies* books of Cicely Mary Barker, verses of gentle whimsy with each flower given its own page, a watercolour in exact detail, and alongside it the picture of a fairy child.

It wasn't clear which was real and which was fantasy. Once I was let out to play, I sorted the truth for myself. I realised that rather than recoil from nature you get pleasure, even fascination.

We lived on an unpaved road just at the point where the houses petered out into fields and hedges. Roaming freely as children were allowed to do in those days, I began to match the *Flower Fairies* book names to the actual flowers that grew in abundance in the fields. I began to search out the more unusual. Later, when we all began collecting things – sea shells, shrapnel from German bombers – I collected flowers. They went from being a part of the free-waving countryside to being specimens under my control, pressed within the grey pages of collecting books, each one labelled and annotated. After just one season I had some fifty different flowers. Memory of them is how today I can still identify scarlet pimpernel and viper's bugloss.

And I marshalled them for my first foray into the literary world. When I was about twelve the children's pages of the local newspaper held a short-story competition: the subject was to be 'The Flower Show'. Mine was meant to mock the way adult shows were all about big blooms, and bright colours – garish dahlias, asters, peonies. Instead my heroine submitted a bunch of wildflowers, harebells, buttercups, scabious, so artlessly arranged with ferns and dandelion leaves that she won first prize. My story won second.

As I grew older, emotional turmoil and intellectual angst took over. I noticed the natural world, but only barely: I loved that the Cambridge Backs were awash with daffodils each spring; I took delight in Newnham's gardens, in part designed by Gertrude Jekyll, of whom I had never heard. But these were accidental pleasures. I saw plants and gardens as other people's achievements, there to admire and approve. I found no way to access the visceral pleasure they clearly give to others. Slowly this began to change.

It began with the need of the spirit to find somewhere to be, a place to rest from the restlessness of life. When I was in my twenties and visited grand houses, chosen for their architecture, their art, I began to notice their gardens. Stourhead, Sissinghurst, Cotehele, Tyntesfield: I walked and was rested. Plants and flowers have no egos. Being present in such places was enough: I noticed neither bud nor branch; I seemed to have forgotten much of what I had once recorded in my childish books, their names, their habits, their seasons. But I knew nature to be my solace.

Then life quickened. And once settled in London my own engagement with gardens dwindled. I had only a small shadowy space, given over to the tenants who rented our basement. It was paved and shabby and unappealing. None of us had been inclined to improve it.

All that is changing. As I make my moving plans, I visit two gardens of famous people, people I admire. First Charleston, the former farmhouse and home of Clive and Vanessa Bell, Virginia Woolf's sister, who welcomed many of their Bloomsbury friends to stay there. Since their day the house and garden have been open to the public year round, and in May each year the Charleston Festival hosts a covey of writers in its copious marquee. The walled garden is then a place of inexhaustible joy, poppies, lavender, an aged mulberry tree, flagged walks, statuary: a place to relish being alive.

The other garden is at Giverny, in Normandy, home of the impressionist painter Claude Monet. He loved it dearly and lavished care on its design and its great variety of flowers: 'all my money goes into my garden,' he wrote. Visiting allows you to view the great alleys of densely banked flowerbeds, colour coded into dense swathes of blues and purples, or reds, oranges and pinks. Somehow this looks quite natural, hollyhocks, nasturtiums, begonias mixing informally with more exotic and rarefied plants. And then there is the water garden: waterlilies of course, and the Japanese bridge so familiar from his paintings. The whole thing fell into disarray after Monet's death, but great efforts were put into catching at the fleeting memories of those who had known him to recreate it exactly as it had been. This is clearly one man's vision. I doubt I can ever become as dedicated.

Britain is a land of gardeners, gardens and garden centres: some fourteen hundred of the last are registered with the Horticultural Trades Association, employing around fifteen thousand workers and contributing £14 million to the country's wealth.

Their customers are some of the eight in ten people in Britain who live in a home with a garden. One in ten of us has access to a balcony, a terrace, a patio or communal garden. The horticultural industry as a whole is worth about £30 billion to the UK economy.

All this enthusiasm takes traditional form in the Royal Horticultural Society, which was established in 1804. Joseph Banks – the botanist who had sailed with James Cook and brought thousands of specimens back to Britain – was among the founders. He would be thrilled with its growth: by 2019 the membership was over half a million, and the RHS has five gardens – most famously at Wisley, but also at Hyde Hall, Harlow Carr, Rosemoor and now Bridgewater. It also runs the Chelsea Flower Show, which annually draws celebrity crowds and thousands of eager gardeners, creating numerous television programmes and traffic jams around Chelsea.

There are plenty of other flower shows, of course, plus the perky Britain in Bloom competition in which citizens with gardens, balconies and window boxes pull out all the stops to triumph over their municipal rivals.

My creation of the studio will now extend to the creation of a garden. If I am lucky it will bring peace of mind and perhaps ensure that my declining years don't decline so fast. And, once again, I will recruit help. I knew at the back of my mind it was important to plant the garden at the same time as the building work because plants take as long to grow as walls. Now that idea comes to the fore.

I need to learn about soil and watering and plants, trees, shrubs, and find someone who knows these things. I need to find a gardener.

I had been in the habit of calling on Sunday mornings at Camden Garden Centre, a local self-financing enterprise that offers two-year training courses – everything from horticulture and retail to forklift-truck operating and bricklaying – and in this way brings job opportunities to, among others, all sorts of people needing training and work. They mostly work full time on the minimum wage and end up with NVQs and QCFs. It is always a pleasure to visit because everyone is so polite, helpful and well informed.

I would go to gather a few pots of herbs for my windowsill, but stayed to enjoy their range of flowers, ferns, trees, shrubs and every kind of garden furniture and statuary. When I asked about finding a gardener they referred me to a colourful patchwork of personal cards on a noticeboard behind the tills. I browsed. How to judge from a melee of sales pitches, many either too casual or too formal, too terse or too florid. I didn't hesitate long, but in the light of future developments I made the right decision: Alison's card was clear, colourful, informative, friendly. And so was she.

Alison had studied garden design at Capel Manor, a London centre for training in a whole range of land-based skills. By which they mean all things that grow, plus related industries such as floristry, agriculture and saddlery. Clearly the course suited Alison's talents: she went on to find success – medals and such – and was now setting up on her own. She comes round and we get on well at once. I have made a wish list of what I would like the garden to include. I yearn for a magnolia tree: my daughter lives in Bristol, which seems to be the magnolia capital of England, and spring visits are a joy. I have noticed a crab apple tree shedding its gem-like fruit on a local Camden pavement. So a crab apple goes on the list, along with roses (once I move in, a friend will make me a gift of a rose called Dear Joan), clematis, ceanothus and a generous run of kitchen herbs.

Alison would create the design and she and her partner Stuart would carry it out. They were now on my team.

If I am to cultivate my garden it will have to be easy maintenance. People who have grown up tending gardens know how to do it. They are nifty with hoe and rake; they have rubber cushions to kneel on. They recognise knotweed at a hundred paces. I have none of these skills: I have a trowel and some green string for use on my bowls and pots. Everything else will be new.

I browse the gardening pages of magazines and watch a few gardening programmes: basically, they are written and made for capable younger people already in the know. (I ask myself, how old is Monty Don?) I don't qualify. But I know I must learn the limits of what kind of garden I can deal with. Flowerbeds will need to be raised so that I can reach the plants, and tend the herbs of which I intend to have many: parsley, thyme, mint, chives, oregano, sage. And probably others I don't yet know of. Can I grow dill? Tarragon? Rocket?

I will need plenty of paved space where I can sit and enjoy the sun, which arrives early, slanting across the six-foot rear wall, by mid-afternoon fills the whole garden with light, then sets, casting dying rays into the studio itself.

Gardening and its aficionados have scarcely been on my horizon. Now I am to explore a whole new landscape of activity. I might even take to regularly watching gardening programmes on TV; though perhaps not.

8

Loss

Now that papers and money are being exchanged, I need to move up a gear. I need to make a serious effort to get rid of a lifetime's furniture and house contents. This will really shake up my sense of who I am.

I realise that growing old involves a change in character. The changes may have their origins in the physical or the mental: a brain that is not as alert, reflexes that aren't as quick, short-term memory loss. These play along with the natural sense of loss and decline. Taken together they can make us grow more wary, even fearful, more anxious about the world in general and about specifics of our own lives in particular. We are all somewhere on the scale of longevity. For many, the older you get the longer you want to live. As Hardy's Tess realises as she contemplates the dates of her child's birth and death, 'there was yet another date, of greater importance to her than those; that of her own death . . . which lay sly and unseen among all the other days of the year'. We each have such a date waiting for us; it will not be gainsaid.

It never occurs to the young that they won't live for ever. Such attitude liberates them to indulge lifestyles that have terrible consequences: imagine what musical riches might have followed had the likes of Jimi Hendrix, Janis Joplin, Amy Winehouse or Kurt Cobain not been caught up in a drug culture that killed them. They went too soon. In earlier times, rampant disease took its toll on the innocent young: what would literature be like if the Brontës – even just one of them – had lived beyond forty? What did the world lose when Keats died of TB at twenty-five, Jane Austen of now-treatable illness at the age of forty-one? Rupert Brooke or Wilfred Owen, gone in their twenties in the foreign fields of the First World War, might have become Poet Laureate. We who grow old not only remember them but count our own years with thanks.

But many remain. Having initially dazzled the world with their youthful brilliance, a whole raft of the gifted continue – out of the spotlight – to enrich their legacy. David Hockney, Frank Auerbach, Bridget Riley are still painting with life-long fervour. Old age need not signal decline, but you need security, opportunity, to thrive. Even then, the world they knew has gone: witness David Hockney's continuing surprise that he is not allowed to smoke even at the opening of his own exhibitions. (A special tent was constructed by the National Portrait Gallery to accommodate his habit without breaking the law.)

The world is moving away from my generation's ways of thinking, built up over a lifetime of habit and engagement. The way things used to be – behaviour, morals, routines – have all been shifting as we have grown old, often with our approval and collaboration. Who would return to the tight hold of class and church that prevailed in our parents' generation? To us as we age that rate of change seems – deceptively perhaps – to be accelerating. I cling on to concepts of civic duty, loyalty towards individuals, probity in finance, and feel the sands shifting under my feet. At the same time concepts I gave little thought to are assuming a greater and welcome prominence: concern for the climate and the countryside, the principles of vegetarianism, matters of racial and sexual equality, issues around abuse and giving offence, acceptance of gender fluidity – all these are now part of the current outlook in the society to which I belong.

While I flounder privately with much of this, and often feel alienated, I welcome its happening. I retire into my shell, nursing what remains of what I once did easily. Now I must marshal tired energies for this one last project in a world grown strange.

I hand my son a strip of small blue sticker-spots, and my daughter a strip of red. They are to go round the house and mark everything they would like for themselves. Soon I am living in a house whose furniture has got measles. My son's blue stickers are most in abundance, my daughter's red hardly at all. Fortunately I have a grandson setting up home in an empty flat. I rush to fill it for him – not always successfully.

I take to the streets, at least to that stretch of pavement at my front door. Each weekend I set up shelves and heap them with unwanted goods. In bright felt-tip I write on a big board: 'FREE: Please help yourself'. Then I hide behind the curtain, watching to see what attracts attention. I have to resist rushing out and saying, 'Yes, nice, isn't it? Made by my mother at her pottery class!' My mother's output of pottery has become a burden: although attractive enough, it isn't the sort of thing you'd particularly favour over, say, a Bernard Leach or a Lucie Rie. The dilemma is, does it have any greater claim on family loyalty than, say, a nice piece from Conran or John Lewis? I seem to think it does. Does the gift of it from me, their granny, passing it from their great-grandmother, have no sentimental value? I sense a good deal of wriggling. So I hear myself saying, 'Oh, please, just take it, will you, and then throw it away without telling me . . .' Family loyalty saved.

Although my house opens directly onto the street there isn't enough passing footfall to constitute any kind of consumer demand. I go on the Nextdoor app and post a message explaining what I'm doing. I get replies: 'What time can we arrive?' Well, it's on the pavement, so any time will do.

Perhaps not before breakfast. And come they do, a steady trickle of people who either fancy a rummage through my stuff or who might actually take things. Every hour I peep out and if there's no one actually there, I go out and refill the shelves. Soon I am wandering round the house laying shelves and cupboards bare.

There remains a good deal of stuff I try to sell; or failing that bestow on a good home. I set about drawing up a list of whom to approach.

I have forty vases: in a cupboard, a high-up cupboard. I forget how they accumulated. But every time someone sends me flowers in a vase, I keep it. When the flowers die, I wash and store it. Rarely do I use it again. 'You never know when they might come in handy': the mantra of my wartime childhood.

The war made us ecologically aware, though we didn't know at the time. We kept things. We didn't throw away. Everything has its re-use value: string, elastic bands, newspaper, vases. Childhood rules go deep: the habits of mind learned then are hard to unlearn. And thrift has served me well. I've been using a linen window blind as a bedspread for years.

As well as the war effort calling on our services, there was the matter of money. Not much of it and not likely to increase. In my day, mothers mostly didn't work – that's how it was phrased. That is, they didn't have paid jobs. They worked unpaid seven days a week at cooking, cleaning, washing, shopping, the same routine over and over each day. They needed to be careful with money; change was always counted.

Everything that could be recycled was: dresses were unpicked at the seams, the fabric washed and ironed and used for another garment. The fashion for different-patterned skirts and sleeves, with inserts and extensions, was born of necessity. Sweaters were unravelled, the wool washed and rewound and knitted again. Squares of different wools were stitched together to make blankets. Nowadays such things feature in craft shops as quaint revivals of old skills. But given the growing awareness of the planet's limited resources, they are reviving. In which case: ask your granny.

That's how I come to have so much stuff.

'You need Fliff,' my friend Rachel tells me. Fliff has already cleared the rooms of several mutual friends: she does it as a second string to her bow. Now she will come to my rescue too. I have a new recruit to my team. A new expert.

Fliff comes round for our first meeting. She is a delight; relaxed and slender, she looks every part the distinguished potter she is, capable but what my mother would call 'arty'. She has swinging long dark hair, which she will over the coming weeks wrap casually in a variety of knots and bunches. She wears easy but stylish artist's clothes: denim smocks or loose dungarees, managing to be informal but stylish. Her gaze is clear and purposeful.

She is kind but firm, setting out how we will work together.

She has an informal but exact routine. 'You will only be able to stand two hours of this at a time: it's emotionally draining!'

For our first session she brings two large cardboard boxes, and one smaller one. She sits opposite me as we confront a pile of books: she holds up each in turn. 'Keep', 'Go' and the smaller box 'Ask'. And into one of the boxes each of the books goes.

This last box refers to the books I think might have a resale value. I decided against dealing with antiquarian booksellers when one of them said my December 1847 second edition of *Jane Eyre* was of no interest whatsoever. My taste was snubbed. I can do without that. So I will go through Fliff, who has a bookseller she will ask to sort things out for us.

At this point I realise that over the years I have assigned a vague monetary value to everything I have. Nothing too precious, but plenty that might well turn up on *Antiques Roadshow*. Some nice pieces of Victorian furniture, usually bought from the chaotic shop down the road which was run by Ron Weldon, the jazz musician husband of the novelist Fay. Lots of books, a good few signed by the authors – 'with love to Joan' – and those forty vases.

I am about to learn a lesson about the abundance of things.

The world is awash with used goods. eBay, the online hub for auctions, was launched in September 1995. By 1997 it had hosted two million such interactions. They'll tell you there's a market for everything: clothes, books, furniture, knick-knacks. Second-hand goods are traded round the world: there are companies in every country making good money clearing out homes, grading the contents and selling them on. Japan has eight thousand such companies: in 2016 its second-hand business was worth $16 million. In the same year it had twenty million used clothing consumers. In 2018, China was a major importer of second-hand clothes; now it's a major exporter.

In 2016, a study sponsored by Marks and Spencer and Oxfam found that British cupboards contain 3.6 billion unworn garments. Between 2000 and 2015 global clothing production doubled and the average time a garment was worn declined by 36 per cent. It's said that millennials discard their clothes after one to five wears. Once-cherished dresses – beautifully hand-made, of sentimental value – will have no value at all when grandchildren try to cash them in.

Books: mostly, they are of no value individually. But bought in bulk they add up to a tradeable commodity. Again Japan is good at this. Even so, Bookoff, its largest used-book buyer, sends thirty-five thousand tons of books to paper recycling every year. Oxfam has the largest chain of second-hand book-shops in Europe, with a hundred in the UK. In 2019–20 they sold eight million books at an average selling price of £2.50, earning over £19 million. As for those that remain unsold, Oxfam has partnerships with recycling companies where the surplus goes for reuse, recycling or pulping. Together they try to make sure the books don't end up in landfill.

Furniture: broadly speaking, antiques have had their day.

Christie's — the UK's foremost auction house — has seen the price of much traditional European furniture fall by as much as 70 per cent in a generation. The price of antiques in the UK market has fallen some 50 per cent in recent years. People no longer want brown furniture when they can have Ikea.

And yet, alongside the trade in mass quantities of things people no longer want, there exists a buoyant market for specific, highly individual items that people rate as worth having. Vintage handbags are a case in point: on eBay they go for hundreds of pounds. Pyrex kitchenware, once the staple of 1950s and 60s kitchens, used by those legendary smiling housewives in frilly aprons, is now rated highly by young Americans. Hummel porcelain figurines, once produced in limited editions to be highly collectable, have both slumped and soared in monetary value. Even odder, to my taste, is the sudden value of items of pop culture. They turn up regularly on eBay. Apparently, a mint-condition *Star Wars* figure in its original packaging can sell for thousands of dollars. Currently, the latest trend in furniture lies in post-war high-end designer furniture from Denmark and Sweden: Arne Jacobsen, Hans Wegner, Greta Grossman and, for lighting, Poul Henningsen.

Clearly the world has enough goods to go round already. It is the matter of distribution that is the problem. And yet our global economy is still premised on the concept of growth.

───※───

Back to my own stuff. Fliff will make many visits. I am always pleased to see her, but she is right about the

two-hour limit. After that I begin to wilt and, worse, lose my power to discriminate.

I begin to ask around to see how others manage. I put the question to a bookish dinner party. Which paperbacks would you turn out: Rex Warner or William Faulkner? Several editor/book-reviewing types offer 'junk the lot', meaning all paperbacks, not just the two in my challenge. Others ask, 'Who's Rex Warner?' I explain his brief success and fame. And fall to thinking, if he isn't known among such reading fanatics as these, perhaps Rex Warner needs me to sustain his now-depleted reputation and I should keep my gnarled orange Penguin paperback for future genera-tions. William Faulkner fares better. Everyone has heard of him and read several. But there is no great feeling he earns a place on current domestic shelves. They make another pertinent point: 'You can always buy a copy if you need it.' In the end William Faulkner goes, Rex Warner goes too.

I have always organised my books according to subject: history, travel, fiction, reference, religion, politics and so on. Now I have to decide where I can cull. Reference books present specific problems. They have been invaluable over the years and I enjoy having them within reach. But they are bulky, take up shelf space. Also, almost everything is now available on the internet; if not directly, then at least through references. Wikipedia is just the start. Project Gutenberg is useful, and all the libraries that have digit-ised their collections. These latter I have not yet accessed, being set in my traditional ways. But moving house is prompting me to update in many areas of life. Digital libraries may be one.

But then I consider the fatal fallout if all books were to become available and read only online, or on a Kindle. Not only would we lose the texture and smell of books themselves, the greatest of snuggle-comfort by a winter fireside or under a puffball duvet, but the world's libraries would lose their *raison d'être*. The idea that they may decay or be repurposed is unthinkable.

The very thought of libraries warms the heart. We think of books as where we can find the world's accumulated knowledge, insight and guidance. Familiarity with them has been one of life's reliable pleasures. As a young graduate I had a card for the original Reading Room of the British Museum, its star-shaped spread of reading tables hallowed by the shades of passed readers: Marx, Wilde, Lenin, Gandhi, Orwell, Shaw, Wells, Woolf, Rimbaud, Marcus Garvey, Conan Doyle. Louis MacNeice wrote a poem about it, Max Beerbohm a short story, David Lodge a novel. Today it is preserved – a haunted hollow, its future 'under discussion' within the glorious spaces of Norman Foster's reconfiguration of the British Museum.

The first free public library in Britain was founded in Manchester in 1653, under the will of Humphrey Chetham, one of the city's first and most successful textile merchants. He insisted it be free of charge and it still is. His trustees set out to collect works that would rival the libraries of Oxford and Cambridge colleges: history and theology featured well; today's acquisitions cover the history of Greater Manchester and Lancashire, a treasure trove for the researching scholar. Chetham also created what was then known as Chetham's Hospital, providing accommodation and education for 'forty poor boys' and later to transmute into the now-renowned Chetham's School of Music. But the old library is still there, its seventeenth-century shelves and stacks, its twenty-four carved oak stools all as they have been for centuries. It holds a special place in my life.

I grew up loving the various libraries I knew; I held them precious because I knew they were vulnerable. I learned of the famous lost library of Alexandria, home of some four hundred thousand papyrus scrolls regarded for centuries as the origins of geography, science, medicine. It was already in decline when Julius Caesar put the torch to it in his ruthless civil wars. More recently the priceless manuscripts of Timbuktu – historic Arabic texts dating from 1204 – were destroyed by fleeing Mali rebels in an act of casual revenge. Such loss haunts the mind.

And not only mine.

Ray Bradbury, in his 1953 novel *Fahrenheit 451*, imagines a future dystopia where 'society as a whole decided to simply burn books rather than permit conflicting opinions'. His hero joins a group of renegade intellectuals known as the Book People, who memorise texts to keep them alive. Knowledge and truth, we know, are the enemies of power and tyranny. Libraries keep their flame alive.

Time to recite aloud Shelley's 'Ozymandias' – learned

by heart more than seventy years ago. Decisions about my own books falter. I am torn. I decide to split the difference, saving only the favourites: Gustav Kobbé's *Complete Opera Book*, *The New Oxford Companion to Music* and Richard Mabey's *Flora Britannica* are among the reference books I save. None is a recent edition, but they are packed with enough knowledge to last out my lifetime. They are old, reliable friends.

Before Fliff came into my life I called my local independent bookseller round to cast his knowing eye over what might be of any value. I showed him with pride my complete set of Dickens: twenty-one volumes, leather-bound, published by Chapman and Hall in 1901. He let me down lightly. 'Do you know how many complete sets of Dickens I get offered?'

But then there is an odd shelf of books treasured for their place in my life. Three volumes of A. A. Milne, the obvious legacy of been born in the 1930s; three volumes of Ameliaranne Stiggins stories, moral tales of a poor child, her virtues and aspirations in a brutally class-ridden world. (The latter is my extrapolation: the author assumed it was the natural, though unhappy, order of things.) And a copy of *The Struggle is My Life* by Nelson Mandela, signed 'To Joan with my compliments and best wishes, Nelson Mandela 15.3.90'. The date is just thirty-two days after his release from prison. I had flown to Stockholm to interview him and taken the paperback with me, and it will stay with me always. My 1911 edition of Charles Kingsley's *Westward Ho!*

earns its survival for another reason. On the inside of the front cover is pasted a formal dedication headed by a coat of arms. Then, in fancy antique lettering, it says: 'Presented by the Feoffers of Chetham's Hospital – Humphrey Chetham's school – to John Rowlands (class 2 B) Special Prize, for Proficiency in Drawing Exercises'. The prize was for my seven-year-old father. He was one of Chetham's 'forty poor boys'. *Westward Ho!*, published in 1855, is wildly out of date, a tale of Tudor derring-do with the profiteers of Elizabethan England fighting and beating the Spanish fleet, in celebration of pioneering Britain's colonial future. It sits oddly beside the Nelson Mandela.

9

Look

E ven if they are merely the canvas of a tent or the inside of a converted van, walls define a home. Anyone who has lived within the same walls for more than a year will surely have put something there: schooldays fandom, student posters, photographs as families disperse, then serious stuff: paintings, drawings, prints, photographs.

Moving on means discarding many: each one is a loss, a wrenching of memories, remembrances of happy times, occasions of choosing, of hanging, the daily glimpse at the turn of the stair, the sense of homecoming when the door opens on expected portraits, landscapes, art.

I am leaving a four-storey house with an attic. That's a lot of wall space. And I love pictures – all kinds of pictures. Anyone trying to assess my taste would be confounded by the mixed messages that leap from my rooms. What is it that governs our taste in art? And what is the link between the range of that taste as an abstract idea and the reality of oils and canvas, drawings, photographs and posters that find their way into our daily lives? The question occurs over and over as I wonder which to dispose of and which to take to the much-reduced space of my new home.

In 2020 Art UK invited me to join their 'curations' scheme, which allows the public to trawl the nation's art collections to select and recommend a number of favourites. I was at a loss: I like too much.

Attempts are constantly made to fire up popular enthusiasm for looking at art. Art UK is just one such. Across the world, collections begun by monarchs or rich benefactors and bequeathed to the nation have fallen into government care. They, declining to make more than a meagre financial provision, tell collection trustees to raise the rest from public and individual support. Hence the proliferation of friends organisations, membership cards and gift shops, all of which raise money. To boost funds further museums and galleries now offer tempting lectures and tours. I still have my tickets for a 2020 tour of the Uffizi in Florence, postponed by Covid, my Royal Academy booking for the Tracey Emin/Edvard Munch show and a twice-postponed ticket for Artemisia Gentileschi at the National Gallery. So much missed leaves me with a real art craving.

A fear lingers at the edges. Many historic collections have come together with money traced back to conquest and exploitation. The modern mood is to expose such legacies. There have long been calls for the return of objects either sacred or symbolic to their country of origin: the

Elgin Marbles, the Benin Bronzes. These calls are growing in number and force. More recently, in the case of slavery there is increasing pressure for museums to display written accounts of their shameful origins and remove statues of early founders from public display. This puts our cultural heritage correctly at the centre of public discourse.

But in changing to meet the demands of today's identity politics, is there a risk these institutions will be destabilised beyond recognition? If each museum returned its collected artefacts, most would be reduced to only their own native-mode objects. How restricted and inward-looking that would be. Then again, the arrival of digitisation, the internet, future interactions as yet undreamed of, will change these places – perhaps they must. That is for younger generations to decide. But I love museums and galleries structured the way they are: so, please, wait till I am gone.

More immediately, I must deal with the almost random selection of art present in my daily life, from huge exhibition-scale posters to graduate work bought at art school shows, to purchases, gifts, photographs, friends' work, all making some kind of sense to me on my walls. It has taken years of affectionate accumulation and idiosyncratic taste to select and arrange what goes where.

What you see and what you observe around you in early life is where we all start. I grew up with a love of the Pre-Raphaelites, because they were there, in front me, and they were easy for a child to love. The industrial north-west of England is particularly strong in them. The suddenly rich industrialists of the nineteenth century wanted to be both philanthropists and proud collectors, so many of them bought and gave to their cities' galleries pictures that were all the rage at the time. Manchester probably has more Pre-Raphaelites than any other genre. I was intrigued by the immediacy of *Autumn Leaves* by John Everett Millais and the complex of activities in Ford Madox Brown's *Work*. These are paintings that tell a story. You know where you are with them.

At school my art teacher had a passion for the Renaissance, conveyed to us via her vast collection of postcards. These told stories too, though in different styles: a mother with a baby on her lap was, for obvious reasons, the most abundant, but there was also a thrilling mix of beheadings, forest hunts, monks busy with books, naked nymphs and courtiers in glamorous clothes. All this nourished my teenage taste and sank deep. Student opportunities opened further: galleries to visit, exhibitions, current episodes of outrage and scandal. The Festival of Britain promoted a touring exhibition of Britain's finest and best. It was the first time I saw a Lucien Freud, *Interior at Paddington*. The Duke of Edinburgh was said to have asked of a Ruskin Spear, 'Is it hanging the right way up? And how do they know?' Clearly modern art would need its defenders. I began to sense a mission ahead.

I took my degree in economics and history, but it was art that fleshed out my imagination: *Napoleon Crossing the Alps*, *The Execution of Maximilian*, glittering monarchs of various sexes, politicians almost entirely male. Poets and writers independent of spirit: Byron in a turban, the Brontës tense and haunted, always there was a narrative. Even landscapes told of wealth or industry: Gainsborough's Mr and Mrs Andrews survey their property, Samuel Palmer's peasants work in Shoreham's fields.

The pictures in my college room were an insight into my naive dreams. Pride of place went to a reproduction of Renoir's *La Loge*: a beautiful woman, fabulously gowned, in a luxury theatre box with an attendant male. On another wall – a seemly distance from the worldly indulgence of the Renoir – was a reproduction of a Flemish Virgin and child, delicate, detailed, but dominated by the tumbling blue folds of the Virgin's robe. I was clearly struggling with how to present myself to the world, torn between the sacred and profane. And I was yet to learn that among the intellectual classes I so admired, reproductions were distinctly infra dig.

Once I had house with a long staircase and tall walls, I indulged my love of posters. Over the years I collected not only reminders of my museum and gallery visits, but gorgeous designs in their own right. An array that told tales of history, archaeology, political rivalries as well as prints of artistic masterpieces. Here was the poster for an exhibition in Bayeux, celebrating *La Tapisserie de la Reine Mathilde*; the Stockholm exhibition poster for the restoration of the *Vasa*, the Swedish warship overloaded with cannon at the insistence of King Gustavus Adolphus that sank on her launch voyage in August 1628, and was lifted from the deep in 1961.

A favourite came from the *Dutch Art in the Middle Ages* exhibition at the Rijksmuseum in Amsterdam: it featured a huge blow-up of a young woman's face, folded into a wimple and magnified many times larger than the small jewel of a painting from which it was taken. Posters can do that: stretch and restructure, even distort, their source material. The same was true of the Rembrandt portrait – in his usually favoured armour – featured in the poster from his exhibition, again at the Rijksmuseum. All these dressed my four floors of staircase. Who would ever want them?

The question hovered over the largest poster of all, a vast blow-up of a detail from a Pinturicchio painting: a man with a halo of blond curly hair beside a glorious horse. The setting seems idyllic until you notice in the background a row of dead men hanging from gibbets on the brow of a hill: treated, as it clearly was, as a common and unremarkable sight outside medieval Italian towns.

There were more: a Henri Rousseau poster from a French exhibition, a Caspar David Friedrich from the Tate and Toulouse Lautrec from the Prague National Gallery. All were loaded with reminders and memories of cherished visits. And yet another told its own strange story.

In the tumultuous middle years of my life I had gone for help to a distinguished psychiatrist, whose steady and insightful conversation saw me through several traumas. Years later I discovered that she had also helped someone who had become a close friend of mine. Each of our conversations with this psychiatrist had, not surprisingly, involved the ambiguous place of women in the culture of the 1970s and 80s.

At the same time I discovered a painter who, it seemed to me, epitomised my dilemmas in a number of paintings. The Danish artist Vilhelm Hammershøi painted women alone, dignified, mysterious, standing or sitting in cool, empty rooms. I grew to love them, not simply as haunting paintings alone, but as saying something I couldn't articulate. Years later, two things happened. My psychiatrist died: neither I nor my friend went to her memorial. Then, in the months that followed, the Musée d'Orsay in Paris mounted an exhibition of Hammershøi's work. We decided to mark the two events as one, travelling to Paris for the day to celebrate the important life now lost to us, visiting the exhibition with the thought of her constantly in our minds and conversation. We knew she would have approved. And now here on my wall was the Hammershøi poster: a woman seated at a table with her back to us, a brown dress with a cream frill at the neck, dark hair, nothing more. Inaccessible. Perhaps it said something about all three of us.

There are London shops that trade in posters, but they want them raw, untreated. Mine weren't. I could hardly have pinned the flimsy paper to the walls, and I thought framing them behind glass was somehow inappropriate. Instead I had them laminated onto board, destroying any commercial worth they might have had.

Were they clearly destined for the skip? Still I clung on, wanting to find a home for them, hoping something might turn up. Plenty did: again I used the Nextdoor app, to tell everyone they were going free. No one wanted the job lot of course, but one or two people called round and carried off single posters in the back of hatchbacks. My architects took one. My daughter took the one of the Joan Baez/Grateful Dead concert at Mount Tamalpais in October 1966, which features a drawing of Pooh and Piglet walking into the sunset. I was reconciled to the rest just slipping away. 'Don't look, don't ask,' I said to myself as others disposed of them for me.

Paintings were another matter. They didn't trace any kind of journey. They had been bought steadily over the years, from galleries and, as I grew to know artists themselves, often from friends. These I would keep. For the rest I called in Bonham's and a brisk, crisp assessor with a pretty German accent came and looked them over. She was exact and unmoved: these were commodities to be traded and she took her (not very wide) pick. Off went an eighteenth-century portrait that would later be a colour feature in their sales catalogue as 'probably a lady of the French court'. Off went the John Piper – an excellent one, as it happened, but not one that warmed my heart.

The paintings I held back were largely the work of artists whom I had grown to know – John Bellany, Albert Irwin, Richard Hamilton – and a whole clutch of smaller prints and watercolours that I knew would hang well together in the smaller spaces of my new home. A series of Rowlandson cartoons lampooning Napoleon would end up in my bedroom; nineteenth-century lithographs charting the northern bank

of the Thames went in the kitchen. Quite how and where the rest would go is a story for later.

———— ∞ ————

Decor is a word that makes me uneasy. First, I had never heard it until I was in my late teens; then it clearly didn't refer to anything in my own life. Also, it's probably French – and that's no help at all. On the other hand the concept has seeded a whole swathe of television programmes in which unsuspecting innocents offer up homes they think need a makeover into the creative hands of decor specialists – interior designers. The results are not always happy, with the victims managing to suppress their shock behind ambiguous cries of 'Wow!' It tells me that moving on can be challenging, risky, but rejuvenating. So I began to dream a little.

I imagined what my studio would be like when it became a home. Much of my own furniture would be there, of course. How odd it is that only on a major disruption – like moving – do you see your furniture in its true light. You suddenly see how the caning has gone on that chair, how the fitted covers don't fit any more; where they do, they have faded in the sunlight. The rugs are frayed, the bedside table has been marked by hot cups of tea, blinds have tilted from the horizontal, the curtains, custom-made, aren't going to fit, the upholstery is splitting on another chair, a leg of a chest of drawers is wonky. In truth I live in a house of ruin and desolation.

The *Cambridge Dictionary* defines decor as 'the colour,

style and arrangement of objects in a room'. No mention of wallpaper, then. In building parlance it includes fixtures and fittings: radiators, lights, light switches, shelving. I'm prepared to be fussy about each of those. But where am I to find the overarching organising force to put this into practice? I go in search.

I don't search far. The answer is almost literally on my doorstep. When at the start of all this my friend Andrew O'Hagan was urging me to take the plunge and buy, he invited me round to his own studio to see what sort of a space it was to live in. I was also invited into another adjacent studio, one belonging to Pauline Caulfield, an artist in woven textiles who works from home. The two studios couldn't have been more different in 'decor': Andrew's bookish, full of colourful paintings, sofas, cushions, objects; Pauline's much plainer, rich in bold colours and big, broad spaces. I took ideas from each of them. But mostly I took from Andrew the idea of recruiting professional help.

Jane Ormsby Gore is an exceptional woman. That's in her own right. But before we come to that, it's worth knowing she is from an illustrious family; her father David was the British ambassador to the United States during the presidency of John F. Kennedy, who was a personal friend. Later it's said he wooed – unsuccessfully – Kennedy's widow Jacqueline, who for obscure reasons preferred Aristotle Onassis. Jane grew up in grand houses, then kicked over the traces in the 60s, cavorting with the likes of Mick Jagger and indulging the fashions of the time. She married the maverick fashion designer Michael Rainey; they opened a boutique, Hung On You — pioneering vintage and Indian clothes — and had five children. Then it was over.

Today Jane is the founder and prime mover of JR Design, who marshals her own natural taste and judgement in making large, dull houses beautiful. I knew none of this. I simply had her phone number. So I phoned. Then I looked her up online.

Most of us take the homes we grow up in for granted, hardly appreciating that someone had deliberately brought this medley of stuff together. To us, growing up, it looks dated and dull. Every young couple wants to start again, to their own taste.

In the 1950s the starting point for young marrieds of the day was the Ideal Home Exhibition, an annual event launched in 1908, suspended during the Second World War and revived with much flourish in the post-war years. By the 1950s it was a national event (it lasted until 2009), showcasing all the new gadgetry then coming on the market, and creating domestic room settings that whetted our appetites for the new spending opportunities. Most of these settings were neat and simple: Ercol wooden furniture, Swedish-influenced dining tables and chairs, fabric curtains designed by Robin and Lucienne Day or Robert

Stewart, that seemed at the time dizzyingly daring. I noted down names, references, took samples.

When I went along in the 1960s there was one setting that defied all this comfortable conformity. It was like a stage set in a country house drama: there were dirty wellington boots in the porch, fishing rods leaning on the door, large earthenware pots in the kitchen, wooden spoons and ladles, books and magazines thrown across patterned upholstery, a phone – not segregated in the cold hall but on its own table beside the sofa. It spoke of drama, life, activity, excitement. No designer was credited, but it spoke of the more relaxed and aspirational world that was to come.

Some two million British houses had been bombed out during the war, and any ideas of decorating or refurbishment had been out of the question. Across the country there was a stoked-up eagerness for the new, shiny, modern, available. And we found it at the Design Centre, which opened in 1956 on London's Haymarket. My generation of aspiring homemakers, keen to reject the taste of our parents, began following the latest designs and styles. The Design Centre would live on until 1994, when trends in style and design had become part of the air we breathed.

Jane comes to make an initial assessment of my home and what it tells her of my taste and style. She has two assistants, her tall daughter Ramona Rainey and the small Celine Jumaili, who rides a high-powered motorbike all across

London. They combine flair and empathy in just the right proportions. They all take a good look at where and how I currently live: the colours, furniture, fabrics – in fact, the decor. From it I suspect they are making assessments of the sort of person I am and how I will want to live in my old age. I am nursing a strong impulse to change a good deal of my way of life, cutting it down to the bare essentials of comfort, warmth, good food, books, music, family and friendships.

There follow organisational matters that I am only peripherally aware of, but they take time and concentration. More planning permission has to be obtained from Camden Council for the changes that are planned for the building. It is Grade II listed.

I am now embarked on several journeys, with architects, with builders – Polish of course, led by the formidable Sebastian Hanc, who runs his own company and I am pleased to discover has 'permanent leave to stay' in this country – plus designers and with gardeners. I have on my disparate teams people I know and like, and I expect will know and like each other. I am sure that completes lesson one in the *Management Book of Easy Planning*. So far so good. The only thing I take care to do is make a list.

Before I move in, I would like to know where each of the following will go:

- Suitcases
- Hats
- Boxes of photographs

- Wine glasses and others
- Carrier bags
- Aprons
- Make-up
- Medicines
- Cleaning stuff
- Buckets
- Clothes drying rack
- Stools
- Record player turntable
- Umbrellas
- Folding camp bed
- Gardening tools

And then I get on with my life, which includes crucial debates about Brexit, from February into March and again in May, in the House of Lords. Attendance is not mandatory, but the debates are well informed, with strong cases against being put by people who know what they're talking about. I am not a speaker but merely an attendant listener, and of course a voter when my party issues a three-line whip. Given that I voted against the whip's instructions at the start of it all – against the clause that implemented Article 50 – my presence is one of depressed resignation. Article 50 was the starting gun that began the now inevitable process of Brexit. I opposed Brexit at the time, signing petitions, making small donations here and there, occasionally marching in protest along Whitehall. And I continue to regret Brexit.

At the same time I am also making two new television series for Sky Arts: *Portrait Artist of the Year* for large parts of May and June, and *Landscape Artist of the Year* in June and July. The stress of matching all these commitments somehow invigorates me. As I switch from the studio to Brexit, from Brexit to television, and from them both to moving house I come to relish the tension. And it is how I come to make my big mistake.

10

Error

Things crop up. They always do. You can bet on it. So why do we behave as thought we are in total control? In old age it becomes a compulsion, a powerful need. Control over so many things in our lives is declining – our health, our mobility, our friendships decimated by deaths – we hang on to what we feel we can still control. It is why old people become tetchy, resentful, full of disapproval of change.

I certainly planned to have this move thoroughly under control: decisions taken, plans going ahead, paperwork done, an excellent team recruited, schedules drawn up. But there's the problem. I have never worked regularly in an office, so I have never really absorbed the fact that schedules exist to be changed. It is known as contingency and is part of the system; it should be written into the plan. It is the part that I didn't allow for in my – as it proved – too-rigid planning. The schedule slipped.

It slipped because things turned up. Earlier in the year a message from the architects, Jill and Malcolm, told me that in lifting the wooden floor Sebastian had discovered that the supporting joists were rotten. They would have to be replaced. They managed to phrase it as though they were asking me. They are that kind of architects, allowing you to think you are making choices when in fact there are none. The joists would have to be replaced. I absorbed the news as a child absorbs an unexpected twist in a story. I did not see it as a matter of extra manual work, man hours, ordering timber, waiting for deliveries: in other words, delays. The colours on Jill and Malcolm's chart shifted. The new chart looked as reassuring as the old. But it was markedly different. I went on with other plans as though they were taking shape in parallel. Except they weren't in parallel any more.

And so it was that I came to set the date for the actual move.

The idea of actually moving in and taking possession of my future home had been guiding my every decision and expectation. It was the rainbow's end, the pot of gold, the finish tape, the summit of the mountain. It was not to be.

I researched and phoned a whole selection of removal firms. There seemed little to choose between them. All of them boasted euphoric testimonials from satisfied customers. Once I had told them the scale of the problem, they all seemed to charge around the same price. There were a couple of outliers: one who obviously only moved thrones in and out of palaces and another who was so temptingly cheap it would not surprise me if they turned up with wheelbarrows. Neither would do. I plumped for safe middle, swayed probably as much as by an appealing name as any solid evidence. Much of a muchness, I expected. And indeed that might be what I got. The fault lay with me and my vaunting expectations.

Wherever you lay your head, that's your home. I was about to put that to the test as two sets of expectations came into conflict. My own concept remained fixed; the schedule moved. I expected to move on my chosen date; the building, decor, garden could in no way be ready for that day. My inflexibility marked my failure as a manager. What's more – and I have checked this out with serious professional managers – one single act of misjudgement, even in a landscape of otherwise shrewd decisions, spells future failure for any enterprise. Whenever you read of companies failing, airlines going to the wall, supermarket empires crashing, it can always be traced by one single basic bad decision. And something else: having made that bad decision, something in the character of the decider makes them unable to change. Not only do we not like to admit we might be wrong, we also feel locked into some inner loyalty to ourselves that makes reason, logic, compromise inaccessible. So it was with my move.

My first mistake was my insistence that I could simply move into one completed room of the studio; the bedroom was the only one that made this remotely possible. I could nest in my own space and run my life from there, with the building and decorating still going on around me. What's more, I could keep an eye on how things were proceeding and be on call if Sebastian wanted to check a detail with me: this pale green paint colour or that, this height for the wall lights or that. I would be killing several birds with one stone. All would surely be well, wouldn't it? The answer was a resounding 'no'.

Completion day it is called, officially. For me it's a massive misnomer. As far as my life and my move are concerned, we are only midway, and the engine is idling even there. Nothing is complete except the nightmare that descends on my life. It wasn't meant to be like this, but it certainly, unavoidably is.

I have sold my house. Everyone is conducting the matter impeccably, except me. Estate agent, architects, planners, builders, movers and buyers: all are behaving as appropriate. I am totally out of line. The trouble is I refuse to admit it. Trouble builds.

Ideally, of course, the removal vans should come and collect and then travel to your new home and unpack. Completion day means the house ceases to be yours and now belongs to someone else. Completion on No. 20 is planned for 26 September. The removal vans will there on the 21st and 22nd. But they are going nowhere I can call home. They are going to somewhere called 'storage'.

My daughter arrives on 20 September. So do lots of other

people. I have been offering various pieces of furniture for sale, and with charities like the British Heart Foundation. It seems they all arrive at once. I see my red convertible sofa disappear in one direction, some nice Victorian furniture in another, discarded shelving in a third. It's like Euston station at rush hour, staged by Pina Bausch.

Cometh the day, cometh the van. We're up bright and early and energised by the prospect of the final push. The urgency of actual events tugs at the last impulse of regret and loss. We walk through empty rooms, the marks on the walls where the paintings hung, the walls still the colours we chose. The stair carpet, woven to my specification, is staying. The rug at the foot, commissioned to reflect its colours and the mood of the house, is coming with me. It will lie, rather incongruously, beside my future bed. And be the reminder of what fun it was years ago, at the Suffolk Craft Fair, to seek out the young rug-maker, invite her to submit designs and make our choice. Sadly there is no label on the back to record her identity. Just my memory.

It's like that all the way: just my memory. Recalling odd and obvious things: children's parties, a tenant scam in the basement, the au pair who set the house on fire, the others who tried on my clothes when I was away . . .

For me it is a milestone. Other people move house all through their lives, from home to home as their hopes and incomes expand. For them it is no big deal: they know the ropes, pack up and move on without fuss. For me it is a very big deal indeed. I am going to where I will live for the rest of my life. It is a closure on my eighty-odd years and an acknowledgement that old age begins here.

I am lucky to have delayed it so long. Many of my contemporaries haven't got this far. Memories of them haunt the house, where they came for drinks and suppers. Others with young children, who then grew into teenagers and still came. The many meals round the big table created for me by my cabinet-maker son, Christmases, Easters, as the children and grandchildren gathered to celebrate. Shrieks of laughter, cries of surprise or outrage no longer reverberate. Now the place is still and silent, awaiting other lives.

But this is melancholy, not sadness. My mind has already shifted its loyalty towards the new home and the future. This whole account is how I am making my place for the years ahead, and for the ending. So these tales of designs and planning, of decor and stuff are merely the anecdotal route towards my final years. It is the acknowledgement that I have lived long, known much and am taking only memories with me. Together with boxes of fading photographs, faces I hardly remember and places I can't recall.

And so to the boxes. The removal company arrives to pack up on one day, then delivers on another. They are completely without sentiment, of course: efficient, even brusque, they go about what is a much-practised routine, packing glass with care, handling big furniture down winding stairs. They work at a steady, deliberate speed, ignoring my nervous flutterings. They want me out of the way. Quite right. We head off to the local café for a relaxing breakfast, leaving them to it.

The imperative for me is to pack into a suitcase all I will need for several weeks in the wilderness, including a holiday weekend to be snatched in Nîmes. This means the most versatile neutral clothes, thin fabrics, easily washed, non-iron, and the most comfortable shoes. Make-up and medical stuff cut to a minimum, everything in tiny bottles. This is not about style or even presentability. It's about survival. It's also, I realise, part of diminishing sequence. I am leaving my large, copious home to move into a studio. On the way I am moving my life into a suitcase. It can't get any smaller than that until my body is finally reduced to ashes and stowed in a marble urn.

The thought is almost a comfort. Indeed there is a strange headiness in being finally at the fulcrum of what is my major change. Liberated from the lavish coil of my past, heading towards the future I am shaping, I am now floating in a strange limbo of having no roots, no abode, I am a traveller in an unfamiliar land. But far from the poet's whimsy, it is local and prosaic.

At three in the afternoon I move into the Marriott Hotel in Swiss Cottage.

This was intended as a moment of completion in itself. The house empty, the future planned, my daughter come up to celebrate. A couple of nights booked long ago in the expectation of sliding gracefully into my new home. But the expectation lies in ruins. The celebration stands. We dine at Bradley's, a small but Michelin-noted restaurant familiar from outings to its near neighbour Hampstead Theatre. We drink toasts, we survey the successes so far. We sleep in the comfort of a hotel where everything is provided. It is vastly reassuring. I am not aware as yet that I will be back here again and again. Indeed hotels will become my way of life, though not from choice.

In fact, between 20 September and 10 November I would sleep in six different beds, none of them my own, none in my own home.

Over short periods of time I enjoy travelling alone: trains, cruises, hotels where I have a corner dining table to myself. I have taken weekends on my own in Prague and Amsterdam, holidayed alone in Libya (Leptis Magna was the attraction and there was as yet no war). I have joined cruises to see the fjords and the midnight sun, a lone passenger amid jollying parties of friends. I enjoy the brief friendships that arise unthreatened by commitment, free of responsibility.

Yet it now felt curiously light-headed to be so footloose. There was the ongoing problem of the small suitcase to meet all eventualities: the brief holiday in the South of France, stays with generous friends who offered their guest spaces for as long as I needed, and various spells in between at the Marriott – plush amenities – and a Premier Inn – basics at their best. I ate at all sorts of times, comfort food adding to my weight, and made new acquaintances at every turn.

It was thus I met Iqbal Ahmed.

Returning to my room at the Marriott with the dust and

exhaustion of the move upon me, I found on my bed, neatly placed to catch my attention, a parcel containing a small volume. The handwritten note was neat and concise. Here was someone who had written a book and wanted me to read it: it was a gift made to me, which is odd because the giver was the hotel's own concierge. The author appeared to be formidably well read and in love with books: quotations from Baudelaire and Proust earn their place. His path to publication has been stubborn and persistent, the copy on my hotel bed shows how hard he tries and how he takes every chance he gets to share his work.

Iqbal Ahmed came to London in 1994 from Srinagar in Kashmir. For the first ten years he struggled to find work and a home. He finally fetched up in the hotel business, and he combined his public front-of-house duties with his private writing. The book, *Sorrows of the Moon*, is his third, and is subtitled *A Journey through London*. Idly glancing through its pages I was caught by its idiomatic style, its easy, almost naive, view of London. I stayed to read more: this was a latter-day Mayhew and, it turned out, acknowledged as such. The poet Ruth Padel had commented 'read it and weep: and be grateful for its subtlety, courtesy and depth'. Iain Sinclair in a *Guardian* review wrote '. . . it appears at first to be wide-eyed and innocent. It soon reveals itself as a Mayhew excursion through the cruel and fantastic city we are forced to recognise as our own.' Praise indeed. I later added my voice, to those of Padel and Sinclair, naming it my choice in the *New Statesman*'s Books of the Year.

So why isn't Iqbal Ahmed a renowned and successful author?

The fact is he is simply unknown to the wider world: he has no literary agent and no established publisher, so no route to publicity, no easy access to bookshops, literary festivals and book signings at social events. His books are published by Coldstream Publishers, which turns out to be a company he created for himself with money he saved for just this purpose, and he manages distribution and publicity all himself. In 2020 he published his eleventh book, *The Art of Hospitality: A European Odyssey*, while trying to keep a toehold in the hotel business.

Other writers have treated hotels as home. Nabokov famously spent the last sixteen years of his life in the Montreux Palace Hotel; Proust passed his summers in the Grand Hotel Cabourg; Jean Rhys spent a winter in the Portobello Hotel. Word gets round. Indeed many hotels became famous for their residents: de Beauvoir and Sartre at the Hotel Mistral, Paris; Joyce, Yeats and Synge at the Hotel Corneille in the same city. Dorothy Parker at the Algonquin. The record probably goes to the Chelsea Hotel in New York, where famously Dylan Thomas, Brendan Behan, Arthur Miller, Arthur C. Clarke, Bob Dylan and Leonard Cohen all took up residence – though not, I trust, at the same time. William S. Burroughs, Alan Ginsberg and Gregory Corso at the Beat Hotel, almost certainly at the same time.

Iqbal Ahmed is in lively company.

11

Arrive

The day of the actual move into the studio arrives. I wish it had been as clear and defined as that suggests, a slick operation between dawn and dusk. Vain hope. In fact it was a dribble of activity, some eager, some creative, some makeshift. But it began badly.

In my eagerness to help around the fringes of the move, I have stowed a random selection of items – a tray, a couple of vases, a box of books, some kitchen gadgets, my briefcase and such – in my Mini Cooper, driven round to the studio and parked in the street outside.

Returning from my calming café breakfast I find the car has been broken into, all the stuff riffled through and tossed everywhere, as if the thief knew what they were looking for. They opened my briefcase in the expectation of a laptop, a tablet, or at least a mobile phone. But my briefcase was empty of such loot, merely full of papers, which are now showered in disappointment around the car. My response was complete indifference. I had bigger things to worry about. Still: not a good start to the day.

The huge pantechnicons deliver their goods. They are moved briskly and unfeelingly by an efficient team keen to get the stuff off their territory and into mine. They are not disposed to ask 'Where should this go?', merely to place it somewhere, anywhere. Bulky furniture does go to designated locations. But mountains of boxes slowly pile up one on top of the other until the highest are almost beyond reach. They block out the light. I find myself a chair and sit hemmed in by them. Each indicates what it contains: books, kitchen stuff, glasses, more books. I wonder how it will ever get sorted. Then with feigned sheepishness (I sense he must have done this often before), the head honcho of the removal team comes to explain there has been an accident. He shows me the lid of the tureen from my grandmother's cherished dinner service. It's in fragments. Something I hardly use and rarely see but has been with me down the decades suddenly matters. It finally freezes me into immobility. I just sit and quiver.

This is my lowest point: the worst moment. As I've grown older, I've continued to believe in my own competence. My self-belief is that I have the capacity to launch projects and see them through. I embarked on the move intending to call up this very skill. But I discover that stamina ages too. While the resolve remains, the actual demands on brain and body prove too much. I reach a point of collapse. And this is it. I am inert, silent, helpless.

Ironically, the team leader returns with sheaves of paper, asking me to sign off that everything has gone well. I demur: how could I possibly know until everything is unpacked? He explains that I can add a rider to the documents, which I do. I know that it signifies nothing, and I will never refer to them for any claims. What I am learning about my moving is that the loss is not merely emotional and psychological but practical. Perhaps it's a universal truth: every move, from home to home, let alone country to country, involves loss and breakages, a book gone, a glass broken, a dress mislaid. To hope for anything other is to aspire to standards of efficiency that are beyond human effort. Witness wars, business, government and beyond. What counts a small move in a small enclave of a big city? But it counts to me. I learn resignation.

Once the man, his van, his cohorts and his sheaves of paper have gone, I, together with a medley of my family coming and going, start the next, and finally rewarding, stage of the move.

Slowly and with little chatter, we begin.

Over the coming days good things begin to happen. I am over the worst. Things slowly get better. Weakened by my collapse I come to depend on others to help me. And they do. One by one the mountains of boxes give up their treasure.

First the books find their place. Fliff and her friend Flea – who likes books and talks about them non-stop – come to help me sort some more to throw out. The main shelves had already been installed by Jane and her team. My son, his wife and daughter take a weekend to sort what is to go where: Proust, Brontës, Austen on the top shelves. Hardback novels on another. Then came history. I simply don't throw history books away: I notice a book called *The Black Death* by Philip Ziegler, published in 1969. It will lie in wait for a future emergency. There are schoolroom catalogues of kings and queens next to scholarly stuff by Simon Schama, Eric Hobsbawm, David Kynaston. Smaller spaces go to travel, short stories, music, letters, then, whoops, here come heavier quantities of biography, poetry and, strangely, religion. Not so strangely, in fact, because for years I presented *Belief* on Radio 3 and got hooked on different faiths' claims on truth, reality and myth. Perhaps as a consequence, or at least as an indicator, I was later to become co-chair of the Humanist Group in Parliament.

In another room, and destined to have a higher turnover, are paperback novels in alphabetical order, from Amis to Woolf, with a shifting array in between. Of these I cherish a particular fondness for the novels of William Maxwell. I had first heard of his work when his *Time Will Darken It* was the inaugural choice of my book group, some twenty years ago. I knew at once he was a fine writer whom I must get to know. Since then the group has opened my eyes and extended my taste in all directions, and their choices dot the different shelves.

Underneath all, the solemn shelves of tall art books: early Phaidon editions in black and white, including one detailing

Ghiberti's Baptistery doors, carrying memories of early student happiness in Florence; exhibition catalogues, dense of text from festivals in Edinburgh and beyond. Guides to galleries from Amsterdam, Madrid, Prague, Birmingham: always weighty to buy, both in cost and bulk, but worth it for many an hour's browsing in the years ahead. Monographs, often the gift of friends: John Bellany, John Keane, Patrick Hughes, Michael Craig-Martin. And single-artist tomes bought on a flurry of infatuation: Sargent, Hals, Duccio. In the winter evenings to come I will sit with them open on my lap and they will refuel a dormant passion.

In another corner of the jigsaw, the pictures wait to be hung. They stand in ranks along the walls, precariously leaning against each other, hard to measure and compare. I need professional help. The inexhaustible Jane introduces me to a young man called Brett. I never find out his surname because Brett quickly makes it clear he doesn't respond to chatter. I gather bits of background: he is Australian-born, studied at an art school somewhere, really enjoys the task of arranging other people's pictures. I glean further shreds: there are long phone calls with many pauses made behind cupped hands. His visits are intermittent, and though he is always cheerful I sense some domestic drama playing out in the background, possibly over the airwaves from Australia. Who am I to know? All this may be my fantasy. He does the job so well that friends ask for his details. But he left without a goodbye once the job was finished. And left no address or number.

The arrangement of pictures is to his taste alone. And I am happy with it. He puts a Hollywood studio photograph of Hedy Lamarr next to a Richard Hamilton, a watercolour by my mother nudging a Rachel Raphael, an Albert Irwin within reach of a Jack Cardiff photograph of Marilyn Monroe. Brett's gift is the imaginative use of space to deploy pictures that aren't of his choosing but the raw material for his professional collage. It not only solves my problem but offers me new ways of seeing things I had taken for granted in my old house.

The jigsaw is close to finished now. And it is clear there are pieces that just won't fit. Eight chrome and leather dining chairs that were high fashion in the 1980s are now too bulky and obtrusive to fit around my dining table. Sometimes design has to yield to other imperatives. I send the chairs to auction and replace them with smaller chairs by Jasper Morrison.

There is still too much stuff. I have a major throw-out of dresses and shoes, taking bagloads to my local charity shop. I pledge never to acquire so much again. But 'it might come in handy one day' is always at the back of my mind – and sometimes at the front.

Cushions: a retail tsunami of cushions of every size and colour. They make safe and cheerful presents too. But do we end up with the ones we would choose? I save two and ditch the rest. One is a cushion cover embroidered by a young grandchild, in the design of an envelope, simply addressed 'Grandma' and with embroidered stamp and franking mark. The other was made by a prisoner serving time in jail, a beautiful gold-thread rendering of Johnny Cash's famous 'Because you're mine I walk the line'. I relish the irony of his choice given Cash's sensational appearance in Folsom Prison, California, and the wildly ecstatic reception he got from the prisoners there.

I like objects that tell a story. Among them my two naive carved figures bought from tribeswomen at a stopping point on the Amazon, a wooden sailing boat from a Chinese craftsman in Xian, a carved wooden hog from an Argentinian street seller. And then there is the garden gnome. A friend arrived to admire my new home. She did indeed admire it. But went away on a mission, returning with a crudely ugly reclining gnome in red trousers and perky pointed hat. What? 'There's simply too much good taste here, and it needs him.' He now reclines beside my fireplace (which has fake plastic logs, so he'll feel at home).

So what is taste? Good taste? Bad taste? It seems to be the cultural side of snobbery. What I have and you have will depend on which social tribe we belong to. I am probably of the urban culture mob, museum visiting, Wigmore Hall fanciers, Conran shopping . . . shading into National Trust membership and Ikea dependence. Any theatrical set designer would be in clover selecting just the background that skewers my taste with a cruel edge of irony. Think how *Abigail's Party*, the 1977 play by Mike Leigh, mocked the aspirational taste of suburban 'young marrieds', as they were then called. We can all be lampooned for the rubbish life has piled up around our living. Moving house is making me suddenly aware of it.

Moving also means incidental loss. I am aware of all the angst of nostalgia, decline, the years passing. What I hadn't reckoned on is the casual loss of small things: the sudden absence of several silver spoons, the never-to be-seen-again travelling rug, coffee jug . . . Had I intentionally disposed of them in my doorstep giveaway or handed them to visiting children, or have they simply vanished? Children's stories use the idea of lost treasures to enchanting effect, *The Borrowers* setting the tone. Somewhere on the planet my lost goods are circulating, being used, enjoyed, or discarded. Perhaps they are already circulating the oceans lodged among plastic scraps or clogging the drains along with mounting fatbergs. No regrets, then, at their going. Only that I should be adding so idly to the world's mounting detritus.

It takes months to settle in. But now each day is a pleasure, if not untainted with worry. I come to depend on online shops to deliver a steady stream of replacements and additions: glasses, gadgets, bookends. In late summer I decide on a thank-you party: Sunday lunchtime in the now-planted garden. It is great to see everyone come together, architects, gardeners, designers and builders, along with supportive friends, the company who have seen me through the entire downsizing process and helped me discover the route to a settled old age.

And then, I am home alone on New Year's Eve. The new curtains have not yet arrived, so the wide tall windows of the studio send out light towards my *Rear Window* neighbours. Clearly they catch sight of me, for there is soon a knock at my front door and there they are – two strangers – with a bottle champagne, wishing me a happy new year. I knew that over a year's confusion, doubts, mistakes and hilarity I have finally arrived where I want to be.

Eighteen months after my moving in, the coronavirus hit. Initially there was general dismay and a rush to search out information. At the same time there was a low-level alarm, even a sort of black exhilaration as we confronted new fears. And a sudden need to learn about things we had never been interested in before: contagion, medical information, social needs and provisions. My selfish thought was to be glad I had already completed my house move. I was now in a place where I lived on one level, where I could be ill conveniently, with a quiet garden to meet up with friends, in a small and quiet backwater where neighbours would offer help if they thought I needed it. And so it proved. As the weeks went by and we went on the street to clap the NHS, the nation's sense of neighbourhood was to be transformed.

Very soon, neighbours were swapping meals; further afield, local communities were organising a cooked-meal service for those living alone. Trapped in isolation I was soon answering my doorbell throughout the day. Soon it was Amazon, local restaurants, Deliveroo. Within my studio I felt the stress of being alone, but the world beyond – whether by Zoom or local generosity – let me know I wasn't forgotten. Now we are emerging from the pandemic there is a strange familiarity in greeting all of them face to face.

12

Remember

Life-changing events conjure the past: churning up the detritus of the years brings back images, impressions, painful jabs of recollection, sudden jolts of remembered pleasures. Nostalgia is a yearning for the past not so much to bring it back, but to remember how it was. I am holding the past in my hands, objects and diaries from long ago prompting memories long buried. I decide to indulge. Memories, after all, are what make a life, whether from fifty years ago or from yesterday. The saddest phrase as we grow older is 'Oh, I don't remember that!' It's why diaries are so precious: when I read accounts of my travels, written in snatched moments under palm trees or over a late-night brandy, I am at first reading of adventures that belonged to someone else and then slowly, caught by some detail of a beach, a hotel, a view, an encounter, I meet myself. Then the delicious warmth of a memory comes alive to be lived again.

I know a pub. Or rather I know of a pub. No, that's not right either. There's a pub I once knew that I saw again the other day. I saw it from a taxi. It broke my heart.

It stands at a busy junction in what's now called Fitzrovia, the area north of Oxford Street between Great Portland Street and Tottenham Court Road that was once the heart of a lively if somewhat debauched artistic life. And the pub was the heart of that lively and somewhat debauched artistic life.

Today it is boarded up: there are panels of bare wood blocking the windows, so no one can peer in to what was once a velvet and plush, though bedraggled, interior.

It lives on in my mind's eye. It had a bare floor and long mahogany bar glittering with all the brass accessories that hard drinking requires. It had little seating: people stood to drink or perched on one of the few leather-covered bar stools. The women sat. An old-world courtesy still prevailed, a sort of louche gallantry that acknowledged their sex and also didn't expect them to buy the drinks. Lunchtimes, when I knew it well, were busy, between twelve and three; it would then be closed until six. These legal opening hours provoked a frenzy of hurried drinking as the afternoon closing time approached. Then the most dedicated drinkers would adjourn to a private club in a cellar round the corner. Most of the drinkers worked for the BBC.

Times were different then. The thought rushed on me as my taxi idled in the traffic jam. In my mind, the fine Victorian exterior was still intact, granite pillars and embellishments brooding over today's slick modern streets. Regret? I asked myself if that was what I felt. Yet I was myself hurrying towards a bright and brittle editing suite in a modish set of offices where William Blake had been born. Skittish girls with long black eyelashes would sign me in, lads in flashy trainers and T-shirts with obscure references would offer me coffee. Today's world of work, and I was part of it.

The taxi nudged forward. In the rain the rushing crowds passed by the dead pub. Had it had a more eventful past, there might have been a blue plaque. Perhaps one of the multitude of London plaques claiming Charles Dickens rested his head here for a week or two.

But no one slept at the pub: Dylan Thomas, Louis MacNeice, Samuel Beckett, Patrick McGee, Harold Pinter, Julian Maclaren-Ross came and drank and talked. And departed. Departed now, in the final sense. And I am left squinting through a rainy cab window into a slice of my past. Even the name of the pub – The George – has disappeared.

I think about the first house I knew. The house that was my home. All the furniture in our living room was crammed together, like big teeth in a neat, tidy mouth. Each item answered a need. The sideboard was made up of two cupboards bookending a series of drawers for cutlery, our family serviettes, each in its own engraved ring. Only later did I learn the correct 'napkins', expounded in Nancy Mitford's 1954 essay about U and non-U usage. In lower drawers a miscellany of twists of toffee (sweets were rationed so every sticky leftover was cherished), table mats and embroidered tray cloths, for use on special occasions with the trays that lay even lower down. Above, the sideboard had a polished series of shelves intended for display. Here my parents had arranged a collection of engraved brass cups with blue patterned inners that were of course never used; beside them a brass coffee pot with a long handle. My parents never drank coffee. Their look suggested an oriental origin, but my parents had never been to the East. The only clue – though intrinsically mis-leading – was the body of a real tiny hummingbird, now stuffed and inside the coffee pot. When my parents weren't around I would lift it out and marvel at its shimmering wings. There was no explanation of its source and I knew better than to ask personal questions. My parents had once been to Argentina – maybe that's where they came from.

The sideboard reached from the door almost to the opposite wall, leaving just enough space for a chair to cut across the far corner. There it knocked up against a small bookcase with, as I recall, *Pears' Cyclopaedia* (regularly in use), Samuel Butler's *Erewhon*, Edward Bulwer-Lytton's *The Last Days of Pompeii* and a pile of dog-eared *National Geographic* magazines, whose pages appalled and thrilled me with their pictures of naked indigenous women.

Breasts were never seen in my childhood. And as a child I was curious.

Crammed beside the books was a pouffe whose brown velvet lid lifted to reveal newspapers and women's magazines. The newspapers were hoarded to help light the fire in the adjacent hearth. A sluggish fire was urged into life by holding a single sheet of newspaper across its front. This we knew to be dangerous. Once, my mother briefly away in the kitchen, the paper caught fire and was sucked up into the chimney, where it promptly lit the soot-lined walls. We rushed outside to see flames blazing away from the chimney top. It happened sometimes to other houses. We just waited for it to die down.

On the far side of the hearth, in an alcove, was the room's most useful piece of furniture: the polished wood table with the treadle Singer sewing machine folded away inside, and opened up almost daily for the sewing of dresses and the mending of torn shirts and sheets. Next came the shallow bay window. On winter mornings – there being no central heating – its low window-ledge would be thick with ice. An early chore was mopping up the melt with a dishcloth. In the bay of the window stood the pride of the household, a radiogram. Within its shiny walnut case reclined the family's entertainment; on the left, knobs that would tune to the three BBC radio stations: the Light Programme, the Home Service and the Third Programme, and on the right a velvet-covered turntable for playing 78s. We had a collection of some thirty records in a black box.

My favourite was Tchaikovsky's Piano Concerto in B flat Minor. It took up both sides of two shellac records.

By now in my mind's eye I am at the wall adjacent to the door where we came in. Here was the largest of all the furniture, the dining table: four square with extending panels that came out only when we had visitors, which was rarely and made everything even more crowded than normal. I played in the space under the table, which had cross-struts that I divided into different dens and hideaways. In later years I would sit at this table to do my homework while my parents, in the two brown moquette armchairs, listened to the radio. Other rooms were too cold.

I know this room is such detail because every weekend and each day of my school holidays my mother required me to clean each piece of furniture, dusting from top to bottom, nooks, ledges, the lot. I did so listening to *Housewife's Choice* on the radio. An apt match. I was learning what was expected of women.

The most nostalgic thing of all I have left until last. I would steal into the sideboard cupboard where, beside the biscuit barrel, was a jar of viscous brown goo: cod-liver oil and malt. I loved it. I stole spoonfuls of it. I missed it when I left. Years later, with a home of my own, I bought a jar. The nostalgia of taste. I have one still. At times of crisis I take a spoonful.

The only time I have seen anything like this room was on Channel 4's *The 1940s House*: I recognised everything about it. What's more, I bought the book of the programme.

Nostalgia, not quite. There is too much misery attached. But we don't always remember happy times. Sadness sticks like glue.

I think about pebbles. Pebbles with clear water flowing over them. How can I be nostalgic for pebbles? The stream was near my home, in a small enclave of countryside called Happy Valley. We would go there after Sunday school and, at risk of damage to our Sunday-best patent leather shoes, track the little stream that ran between sloping banks. Across from our side of the stream was a small hill with a grove of silver birch trees on top. We called it Hundred Acre Wood (A. A. Milne's influence lingered in many lives. In the *Newsnight* office of the 1980s Jeremy Paxman was always known as Eeyore). There was a fallen tree trunk across the stream: on brave days and in other shoes we would venture across. These were exploits of childhood daring. They prompted fears of home-coming punishments. So the images remain vivid. Most vivid was looking down from the height of the tree trunk to the clear rippling stream below and the coloured pebbles on the river bed. Lit by the glancing sunlight they had the glitter of gems. I watched them change from minute to minute, varied by the light and the water.

These were moments of pure happiness lived in the complete present of childhood days. Since then I have sought them out in rivers across the world and snatched at the long-ago moment: tributaries of the Loire, upper reaches of the Thames, a stream in Dorset where ducks are patrolled by a single goose.

Today, the image helps me go to sleep.

And then events. Some were so fraught with excitement and tension I don't remember them at all. Two weddings have been and gone. Two children born: I remember the experience of childbirth – who wouldn't – but I'm not nostalgic for it.

The growing-up of children is one perpetual golden memory, but only when they're adults and you have forgotten the snotty noses, the tantrums in the supermarket, the high temperatures in the middle of the night, the slammed doors, the sulks at not getting their own way – all those moments when you could happily brain them. But fleeting moments persist: the pang of toddler sadness as an ice-cream cone fell in the dust, the sweet smell of cuddles at bedtime, the first school uniform, iron-pressed and too big.

But what to make of it all? Is it nostalgia for what had once been? Or is it for what I myself had once been? And who wants to return to their younger, clumsy self? Time passing brings loss, regrets, change; we are left with memories, often unreliable. But who wants memories to be reliable? We are, after all, making them up as we go along. What lingers in the brain is how we feel, not what goes on. One day I may recall even this hectic pandemic time with a sense of loss and melancholy.

EPILOGUE

Belong

I've come a long way. Over eighty years of life; over eighty years of history. What you might call a short century. So let's call my life a short century. My childhood and prime through the twentieth century, a time of great global wars, shifting power games, emerging claims for the individual; my older years in the twenty-first century shaping up as a time of climate and immigration crises, querulous politics and frustrated individuals. My life includes both, has run parallel to both. How much are we all trapped in our times? And how is that shaping how I grow old? How am I now, at the end of a short century, to make sense of a world that I no longer recognise as familiar?

As I child I simply accepted the world around me. I sensed I was born into a confident country: Britain in the 1930s knew itself as important and powerful, the head of a mighty empire stretching from India to the Caribbean, from Canada to the Pacific islands. Its sense of self-righteous superiority somehow infected even the modest homes of industrial Manchester, the aspiring suburbia of Stockport.

Life was conformist: I looked around and saw that men went out to work, women stayed at home, keeping house and raising children. People had jobs for life, a steady wage. Weekends were time off; Saturdays for football pools and visiting, Sundays for church and nothing else: shops, cinemas and such were all closed. I remember this rhythm of life clearly: it felt safe and eternal.

Even the furniture around me – the three-piece suite, unlined curtains, aluminium saucepans, washing line, coal hole – were much as our neighbours had. Our behaviour was much the same too: children did as they were told. If I didn't, I was smacked: a slipper, the back of a hairbrush. Everyone in the family ate the same meals; vegetarians were cranks. Schools too instilled discipline; Sunday school blessed it with sanctity. We were easily scornful of those who didn't conform. I didn't recognise it as a place of limited horizons.

Within this predictable space I found a way to read books, to make friends, to wonder about the world beyond. Facts meant acceptance: the pink map of empire, triumphant dates of British history. But my imagination ran free: tales of heroes, adventures, love and loss. Above all poetry, sharing unspoken feelings, troubling thoughts.

For my generation these early years satisfied childish needs: close families, close communities. There were fears, too, of course. Poverty was close. But I never saw displays

of flamboyant wealth. (An exception was the Dockers –
Norah and Sir Bernard – flashy 1950s socialites reported
in the papers, revelling in tasteless wealth, who were held
in a strange and curious awe.) And for everyone the countryside was never far away. At weekends I watched cyclists
and hikers routinely heading out towards the hills; as a
teenager I would join them. All this seemed in some way
the natural order, the norm. And thus in some way the
crucible of virtue. Perhaps it was a nostalgia for this that
surfaced decades later as the country split over Brexit, and
Brexiteers spoke of getting back to how things had once
been: blue passports, imperial measures.

The world seemed as if it would never change.

And then came war. And growing up.

We children embraced a fierce patriotism: my country,
right or wrong. And we obeyed. The habit of obedience
was a matter of life and death: no chinks of light at the
windows, no loitering in the rush to the air raid shelter,
no telling where my RAF uncle was posted. It became the
habit of a lifetime: obey, unless there was a good reason to
disobey. Now, growing old, we obey doctors, the taxman,
the authorities. We wait to be told how to live our old lives.
Without advice from people who know things, we feel we
will be lost.

I remember the euphoria of victory, the dancing in the
streets, the lights in shops and streets going on again.

I floated on a cloud of happiness: evil had been routed;
the future would be golden. My teens were dawning,

hormones were lively, and all things seemed possible. Indeed many things were possible. A new world order had to be built. My mood was shared in common as the country unfolded from its terror. The sense of rising expectations infected everyone. They returned a Labour government that promised a welfare state. We not only wanted to make the world a better place, now war was gone, but we knew it was possible. And it was our turn.

State-educated children became the first in their families to go to university. I was one. We thought we'd gone to heaven. Rationing ended while I was at Cambridge. We could buy clothes and foods we'd only dreamt of. Homes suddenly had fridges and washing machines. Tourism took off: in the early 1950s I won a travelling scholarship that exposed me to the strangeness of Holland and Belgium. As a student I reached as far as the exotic life of Italy and Spain. Any further seemed unimaginable. In 1957, prime minister Harold Macmillan told the people they had 'never had it so good'. Optimism pays off, and there was good reason for it. As we hit our twenties my generation began to afford their own houses. Drab interiors gave way to the design revolution. We enjoyed making our homes colourful, food took on a continental flavour. We grew into a European outlook. Living among all this we saw opportunities there for the taking. It felt like an amiable and improving society.

Is this a golden age, or a golden memory? It certainly felt good. But our outlook was set against limited, even parochial horizons. In the wider world the Cold War was dividing the Soviet empire from the West. We heard of gulags imprisoning untold numbers of dissidents; attempts to break free triggered ruthless suppression. But it all seemed far away. Not many of us travelled great distances. One or two Hungarian refugees from the Russian invasion arrived in my broadcasting orbit with tales to tell. But the world's concerns didn't ruffle our complacency.

And then change quickened. The artist Bridget Riley called the 1960s 'the party at the end of the war' and there was much partying. With all the fun went loose clothes, loose hair, loose morals. There was great music and available drugs. The most important drug of all was the pill, giving women control over their lives. Many of us wanted to be happy and were.

Soon the greatest social change of the century was gathering strength: feminism. The landmark book for me was Betty Freidan's *The Feminine Mystique*. The scales fell from my eyes. Why, I wondered, were many of my fellow graduates from Newnham College, founded to promote and champion women, now embracing domesticity, with some gentle part-time work on the side? Was I doing that too, and why?

Feminism has, over the decades, had many guises. There was a flurry of conferences in the 1960s passing resolutions, expressing solidarity, but all that activity seemed to belong to the younger generation. I was discovering a much older story: I looked back to school friends whose aunties had been suffragettes; I knew of the struggles for women to become doctors and MPs. I rejoiced that the Elizabeth Garrett Anderson Hospital was created and staffed entirely by women, and dedicated to the health of female patients. I recalled my reading of Victorian novels; Jane Eyre's cries for equality with men, the frustration of *Middlemarch*'s Dorothea, trapped in a marriage to a self-regarding pedant. Further and further back I traced the story: Mary Wollstonecraft and Aphra Benn, the painters Vigée Le Brun and Angelica Kauffman . . . soon I was consorting with Elizabeth I, Mary Queen of Scots, Nefertiti and Hatshepsut. For my television programme *Late Night Line-Up* (I was the one female presenter among a churning roster of men) I was sent in 1968 to New York, where I interviewed Gloria Steinem and shared the first stirring of her feminism. In the late 70s the American artist Judy Chicago created a vast tablecloth with place settings for thirty-nine outstanding women. Feminism was claiming its place in law, in government, in matters of health and justice and employment.

We should have rejoiced, then, that a woman became prime minister. Margaret Thatcher was elected in 1979 on the promise of curbing rampant union power and drove forward policies shaped by male ideologues: Hayek, Alan Waters, Keith Joseph. The state was to be curbed and the unshackled forces of capitalism could let rip.

Many of us who were thriving under the old way of life found this abhorrent. We saw it as an attack on civic values and shared social responsibility. We saw the rush to money as a distraction from the central role of society to provide its citizens with homes, food and education, principles instilled during the war years.

Tony Blair's three election victories did something to restore the balance. But New Labour kept up the free-market economics. At the same time, it improved social life: the minimum wage, expanded universities, action on poverty and early-years support, devolved governments. It felt that all generations had a sense of being cared for. Ed Miliband, as Labour leader, asked me to become a working peer and I arrived in the House of Lords in 2011. By then, the political pendulum swung back again into the age of austerity under the Cameron/Osborne axis, and took a plunge into chaos with the Brexit showdown and the confusions surrounding a government and prime minister with little talent and few evident principles.

With the Brexit vote came a major move in global thinking. Brexit was sold to the British public under the banner 'Take Back Control' and struck a chord with those millions who felt that the good things in life had left them behind. In many respects they were right: former industrial areas had declined and nothing substantial replaced the secure jobs that had underpinned a cohesive community. The loss had been painful. And, running as it did parallel to an explosion of consumerism, it generated hurt, resentment and anger: a happy hunting ground for political extremists.

All my life I have marched. I feel a great sense of purpose expressed whenever I take to the streets with fellow spirits. I first marched in 1956, in protest at Britain's invasion of Egypt to secure the Suez Canal, a catastrophic venture that marked a turning point in colonial history. I marched under the Ban the Bomb banner to protest at Britain's nuclear warheads. I missed out – regretfully – on Greenham Common, but was back on the streets protesting Blair's planned invasion of Iraq, Trump's promised visit to London. I visited the Occupy London protest outside St Paul's Cathedral early in 2012, giving my tacit support but interested in the clash between peaceful protesters and the authorities of a Christian church calling in the police to clear them away. I have joined marchers wearing pink celebrating Gay Pride, and green, white and purple for the Women's Movement. I have a visceral sense that peacefully protesting in public is an important reminder of our democratic principles. Now in my late eighties I am feeling too old to be out there with Black Lives Matter and Extinction Rebellion. But I salute their spirit.

At the same time others are marching, and in a different direction. That is their right, but I am alarmed by the demagogic populism that has taken hold in Hungary, Poland, Turkey, the USA. It seems fuelled by passion rather than reason; built on hatred rather than hope. This is a new world I don't recognise and don't like. The continuing refusal of Donald Trump and the Republican Party to recognise the legitimate election of Joe Biden as president in November 2020 and the further intensifying of that refusal

in the 6 January storming of the Capitol indicates a growing confrontation in America between traditional liberal
values — values that derive from the Constitution — and
the forces of populism and violence. I sense that force of
insurrection simmering within many communities in many
countries. Politics are increasingly driven by anger and
resentment. Something within the human spirit is being
badly distorted.

My generation lived with the swings of the political pendulum between left and right, but there had always been a
faith in the system to hold us in equilibrium. The extremes
of wealth and poverty have increased to a scandalous
extent. But many of us still retain those early principles of
civic responsibility and mutual support from our youth into
our old age. Sadly, we sense they are no longer central to
our culture. The world as it is, is not how we once hoped
it would be. For some of us a melancholy sense of disappointment haunts our old age.

I settled into my final home in the months before the pandemic struck. I remained alone and isolated there day after
day. I was changed by it; we all were. The sense of home as
a place of safety grew in power. Many used their isolation
to tinker with their surroundings: walls were repainted,
shelves reordered, attics insulated. We were like small
furry creatures lining our nests with feathers and moss.
Almost daily I fussed about some detail. I walked up and

down. I appraised the comfort. I was pleased and glad. But I yearned for company.

Slowly the country has been growing out of the pandemic. What will we have learned? To value silence, birdsong, clear air; to cherish friendships, family, music and books. To be adept at connecting on the internet and via social media. But most profoundly we realise we have missed humanity itself: faces, voices, noises, movement, connection. We are living in a time of choice. Could the new challenges facing us revive some of my earlier dreams of a fairer and more equable country? What can we now make better in our lives and homes?

The question brings me full circle.

Acknowledgements

What a pleasure it is to thank all those who helped me along the way. They were each part of my life as I moved house, long-standing friends who had always been there, together with sudden and new friendships that, if you are lucky, make any new enterprise easier.

As with my downsizing move, so with this book: the same people who helped with the one have helped me recall the other. Dates, details, accuracy of memory and judgement have all been checked out with David Birkett, Malcolm Last and Jill Pacer, Sebastian Hanc, Andrew O'Hagan, Jane Ormsby Gore, Ramona Rainey, Celine Jumaili, Anthony Pins, Graham Mendoza-Wolfson, Alison Worster, Stuart Hull, Fliff Carr.

Beds and comfort were supplied at short notice by cherished friends Liz Forgan and Gail Rebuck. Writer Iqbal Ahmed has been monitoring the progress of this book along with his own. The artist David Gentleman took generous trouble in rendering the difference between my two homes. Peter Bailey supplied kindly images of my own progress. From start to finish my children Matthew and Harriet have listened, suggested, consoled, provided respite . . . and carried boxes.

The whole enterprise came to fulfilment under the care of London's doyenne editor, Lennie Goodings, with strong support from Zoe Gullen, Louise Harvey and Susan de Soissons: a terrific team.

I have been supported, too, by the numerous experts and authorities who, on the end of a phone, or an e-mail, set me right as to how the world of moving and housing old people currently works. It is a subject that needs further attention . . . but that is a different book.

Credits

Epigraph   Deborah Eisenberg, 'Taj Mahal', *Paris Review*, no. 214 (fall 2015)

50–1   Quotations from James Hamilton, *Arthur Rackham: A Life with Illustration* (London: Pavilion, 1990)

147   'I Walk the Line' lyrics by John R. Cash. Copyright © Stb Music Inc., KMR Music Royalties II SCSP.